GOOD HOUSEKEEPING

COMPLETE BOOK OF
CHOCOLATE

COMPLETE BOOK OF
CHOCOLATE

EBURY PRESS
LONDON

Published in 1993 by Ebury Press
an imprint of Random House UK Ltd
Random House
20 Vauxhall Bridge Road
London SW1V 2SA

COOKERY NOTES

Follow either metric or imperial measures for the recipes in this book as they are not
interchangeable.

Use size 2 free-range eggs unless otherwise stated.

The young, the elderly, pregnant women and people with immune deficiency diseases
should not eat raw eggs (in mousses, etc.) due to the possible salmonella risk.

A number of recipes call for cake crumbs – use home-made sponge cake or shop-bought
Madeira or chocolate sponge and crumble it finely between your fingers.

Where reference is made to a microwave, use a 650-watt oven with a turntable.

Catalogue record for this book is available from the British Library.

ISBN 0 09 177704 6

Photograph on pages 118–9: Charlie Stebbings

Photography: James Murphy
Cookery Editor: Janet Smith
Editor: Helen Southall
Design: Janet James
Stylist: Róisín Nield
Food Stylists: Janet Smith, Emma-Lee Gow

Typeset by Textype Typesetters, Cambridge
Printed and bound in Singapore by Tien Wah Press

CONTENTS

INTRODUCTION

Chocolate is a consuming passion for many of us. Although nutritionists agree that its high fat and sugar content make it exactly the sort of food we should avoid, its unique, melt-in-the-mouth texture and inimitable flavour are irresistible.

Chocolate was probably first consumed as a drink, by the Aztecs in Central America, and it was introduced to Europe as such by the Spanish explorer, Don Cortes, in the sixteenth century. At different times in history, chocolate has been used as an aphrodisiac, a ceremonial refreshment, and even possibly as a currency.

Chocolate quickly became a popular drink in Spain, Italy and France, but it was not until the end of the sixteenth century that it was introduced to Switzerland, now thought of as the chocolate capital of Europe. Finally, in the middle of the seventeenth century, chocolate became known in the coffee houses of London. The popularity of chocolate as a drink spread and new 'chocolate' houses were opened, despite the fact that it was a rather bitter-tasting, heavy brew, thick with cocoa butter.

In 1828, a Dutchman, Coenraad van Houten, discovered how to extract a large proportion of the fat (cocoa butter) from cocoa to produce a dry, powdery substance – what we know as cocoa today. Twenty years later, Joseph Fry, of Bristol, made the first eating chocolate by combining cocoa butter with chocolate liquor and sugar.

CHOCOLATE PRODUCTION

Both chocolate and cocoa are made from the cocoa bean which grows in pods on the cocoa tree (botanically known as *Theobroma cacao*). These lush green trees originally grew in the Amazon Forests – they need moist, humid conditions and short dry seasons to flourish. Today, the trees are cultivated mainly in Africa, Brazil and Malaysia; the beans are exported all over the world.

After harvesting, the large pods are split open and the pulp and seeds scooped out. This mass of beans and pulp is piled up on banana leaves and left for a week or more to ferment in the hot sun. During this time, the pulp becomes liquid and drains away and the beans begin to develop their characteristic chocolate flavour. After fermentation, the beans are dried and it is in this sun-dried state that they are exported.

Once inside a processing plant the dried cocoa beans undergo several more treatments until all that is left is a thick, chocolate-coloured mixture known as chocolate or cocoa 'mass' or 'solids'. This is then pressed, blended, refined and conched (a process which pummells the chocolate backwards and forwards for several hours or several days). The end product of all this is chocolate as we know it.

In its purest state, chocolate is so bitter that it is virtually inedible unless blended with other ingredients. In this unsweetened form, it is traditionally included as an ingredient in several savoury dishes, notably *mole poblano*, the Mexican speciality of turkey cooked in a sauce of chocolate, chillies and nuts. In Spain, bitter chocolate is included in a sauce for spiny lobster.

TYPES OF CHOCOLATE

In these days of manufacturing wizardry, it's no surprise to find that chocolate comes in a variety of forms. The type of chocolate you choose will dramatically affect the way you use it, and the end result. There is no question that the more expensive continental brands, containing high proportions of cocoa solids, give the most intense flavour. These are the best choice when making special mousses or gâteaux. Other types have their own characteristics, as outlined below.

UNSWEETENED OR BITTER CHOCOLATE
This contains about 50 per cent cocoa solids. As the name suggests, it does not contain any sugar. It gives a very strong chocolate flavour and is used commercially for baking and confectionery. It's not generally available in the shops but some specialist suppliers may stock it (see page 157).

COUVERTURE CHOCOLATE
If you want a really professional, glossy finish to confectionery and chocolate decorations, or a very intense 'quality' chocolate flavour, then couverture gives the best result. It contains no fat other than naturally occurring cocoa butter and a very high proportion of cocoa solids. It will need tempering (see page 21) before use if you want to use it as a coating for confectionery or biscuits. However, if you're using it in a cake or mousse, or in anything where it is mixed with other ingredients, it can be used in the same way as any other chocolate. It is available in milk, plain and white varieties.

BAKERS' CHOCOLATE
This is couverture chocolate with vegetable fat added so that it doesn't need tempering. It is easier to use than couverture, but lacks the rich chocolate flavour of couverture and does not give the same crisp, glossy finish. Bakers' chocolate also has a higher sugar content than most couvertures. It is used commercially in baking and may be available from specialist cake decoration and baking suppliers (see page 157).

PLAIN, BITTERSWEET OR SEMISWEET CHOCOLATE
Many brands of chocolate come within this category, all containing varying amounts of sugar and cocoa solids. Most bars of plain chocolate sold in sweet shops and supermarkets contain about 30 per cent cocoa solids, while more expensive brands sold in speciality shops, delicatessens and food halls may contain as much as 60 per cent. Most plain chocolate is interchangeable in cooking, but those with higher proportions of cocoa solids do give a richer chocolate flavour.

MILK CHOCOLATE
This contains sugar, milk solids and vanillin, as well as cocoa solids. Like plain chocolate, many brands vary within this category, but the best contain higher proportions of cocoa solids and real vanilla. Milk chocolate is very sweet and creamy, and not as intensely chocolatey as plain chocolate, so it is most suitable for use as a topping or decoration.

WHITE CHOCOLATE
This contains cocoa butter (rather than cocoa solids), milk solids and sugar. Avoid brands that contain vegetable oil as they do not usually have the true taste of chocolate. White chocolate will not set as solidly as dark chocolate and can be difficult to use. Take extra care when melting it.

CHOCOLATE FLAVOUR CAKE COVERING
This is made from sugar, vegetable oil, cocoa, emulsifier and flavouring. It is available in plain, milk and white flavours. It doesn't have the true taste of chocolate so we do not recommend it unless specifically asked for in a recipe. However, because it is a very stable, easy-to-handle product, we found that, when we mixed it in equal

proportions with couverture chocolate, it was the next best thing to using tempered couverture chocolate for making confectionery and decorations (see page 21 for more information on tempering). The emulsifiers and vegetable oils in the cake covering make tempering the couverture unnecessary. The disadvantages are that the flavour is less intense and the finish less crisp.

COCOA POWDER

A small quantity of cocoa powder imparts a strong, bitter chocolate flavour. Cocoa powder does not contain sugar, so some sugar is usually included in the recipe.

Cakes and desserts made with cocoa powder will not taste identical to those made with chocolate; cocoa contains a relatively small proportion of cocoa butter and therefore lacks the buttery richness that comes from chocolate. However, it is easier to work with than chocolate since it does not require melting and is usually simply sifted with other dry ingredients.

DRINKING CHOCOLATE

Brands vary, but most drinking chocolate contains a mixture of cocoa and sugar. Some brands also contain dried milk powder. These are unsuitable for cooking since the cocoa content is low and the flavour mild; drinking chocolate is most often mixed with hot milk to make a warming winter beverage.

ORGANIC CHOCOLATE

This is a really dark, bitter chocolate made from 70 per cent organic cocoa solids, brown cane sugar, vanilla and soya lecithin (as an emulsifier). Organic chocolate is produced from cocoa beans that are grown without the use of fungicides, insecticides and chemical fertilisers.

CAROB

Not truly chocolate, carob is made from the large, dark brown beans of the carob tree that grows in the Mediterranean area and the Middle East. The beans contain a sugary pulp which is dried and ground to produce a chocolate-coloured powder or confection. It has become popular as a substitute for chocolate, especially from a nutritional point of view, as it contains less fat than chocolate and no caffeine. It lacks the flavour and texture of the real thing and reacts differently when used in cooking. It is not interchangeable with chocolate or cocoa.

Is Chocolate Really Bad For Us?

For most people, the pleasure of eating chocolate is frequently spoiled by a feeling of guilt. Is it really bad for us? Since chocolate contains high proportions of fat and sugar, it is exactly the sort of food we should all be cutting down on, and although it contains small amounts of calcium, iron, and the vitamins A and B, this is not enough to commend it nutritionally. It is worth noting, however, that the finer, darker, more expensive brands of chocolate (with a high cocoa solid content) are lower in sugar and fat than cheaper brands. These specialist brands also have a stronger, fuller flavour, so there is a tendency to eat less.

Carob has a better nutritional profile than chocolate, since it contains less fat and sugar and no caffeine. However, most real chocolate lovers would agree that when it comes to taste, carob doesn't compare. Real chocolate deserves its place in the diet for pleasurable rather than nutritional reasons.

TECHNIQUES
WITH
CHOCOLATE

STORING CHOCOLATE

Both chocolate and cocoa quickly absorb other flavours and odours, and should be stored tightly wrapped in an airtight container in a cool, dry place. Before using in cooking, allow chocolate to come to room temperature still in its wrappings, or it will attract moisture. White and milk chocolates contain a high proportion of milk solids, so they do not keep as well as cocoa and dark chocolate.

Kept at a temperature of around 10°C (50°F), all chocolate should stay in good condition for about a year. If stored incorrectly (in too hot or too humid conditions), the cocoa butter or the sugar crystals in the chocolate may rise to the surface of the chocolate and become visible as 'bloom' – a dull, whitish film. Chocolate that has developed bloom is still edible.

Plain, milk and white chocolate can be frozen providing it is wrapped tightly and thoroughly so that no air can circulate around the surface of the chocolate. It should be thawed at room temperature, still tightly wrapped.

MELTING CHOCOLATE

Break or chop the chocolate into small, evenly sized pieces and put it in the top of a double saucepan with any other ingredients as specified in the recipes. The bottom pan should be three-quarters full of gently simmering water. If you haven't got a double saucepan, put the chocolate in a clean, dry, heatproof, preferably glass, bowl, and set it over a saucepan that's about one third full of gently simmering water. The bowl should fit snugly over the saucepan so that no steam can escape round the sides. The base of the bowl or top pan should not touch the water below. Heat the water gently but do not allow it to boil – a glass bowl enables you to see any tell-tale bubbles. Leave the bowl on the pan until the chocolate looks melted. Remove the bowl or pan from the heat and gently stir the chocolate until it is completely melted.

The temperature of the chocolate should not go above 50°C (122°F). If water or steam come into contact with the chocolate, the texture will be spoilt and the chocolate will 'seize', that is turn into a solid mass that will not melt.

MELTING CHOCOLATE IN A MICROWAVE OVEN

Break or chop the chocolate into small pieces and put it in a clean, dry bowl. A glass bowl is best because it conducts the heat from the chocolate as it melts, and reduces the risk of over-heating. For small quantities, it is safest to use a LOW or MEDIUM setting. For larger quantities, and once you become more experienced, use HIGH.

The table below should only be used as a guide because melting times vary according to the brand and type of chocolate, the initial temperature of the chocolate and the size and material of the bowl used. Check the chocolate frequently and prod it with a spoon – it may look solid when in fact it has melted. White chocolate will burn more easily so watch it very carefully.

Watchpoints

● Use a HIGH setting for Chocolate Flavour Cake Covering (it will melt in less time than given in the table below)

● The addition of other ingredients, such as butter or liquid, will shorten the melting time

Approximate melting times in a 650-watt microwave oven

QUANTITY	LOW	HIGH
50 g (2 oz)	5 minutes	2 minutes
75 g (3 oz)	5 minutes	2 minutes
125 g (4 oz)	5 minutes	2 minutes
175 g (6 oz)	6 minutes	2 minutes
225 g (8 oz)	6 minutes	2½ minutes

MAKING CHOCOLATE DECORATIONS

Chocolate decorations add the final embellishment to many cakes and gâteaux. Most can be made in advance and stored in the refrigerator or freezer until required.

LARGE CHOCOLATE CURLS AND CARAQUE

Spread melted chocolate in a thin layer on a marble slab or clean, smooth work surface, or the underside of a large, smooth baking sheet. When the chocolate is *just* set, push a clean stripping knife (a decorators' tool used for scraping off wallpaper) across the surface of the chocolate at an angle of about 25° (see above). If the chocolate doesn't curl, but breaks, then it has set too solid. Scrape it off and melt it again. We suggest that you buy a stripping tool and keep it for this purpose. A large, very sharp knife can be used instead but it doesn't make such large, fat curls. Smaller chocolate curls made with a knife are known as caraque.

To make two-tone chocolate curls, pipe or spread alternate lines of contrasting chocolate on the surface. Smooth with a palette knife so that the lines of chocolate merge together. Proceed as above, working across the bands of chocolate.

The curls or caraque can be kept in an airtight container in the refrigerator, interleaved with greaseproof paper, for at least 2 weeks (white chocolate) or about 4 weeks (plain chocolate). They can also be frozen.

SMALL CHOCOLATE CURLS

Using a large, thick bar of chocolate at warm room temperature (if the chocolate is too cold it will not curl) and a sharp swivel-type potato peeler, shave off curls along the length of the bar. For narrow curls, use one of the edges of the chocolate bar (see above); for fatter curls use the smooth, flat underside of the bar. If the curls crack as you shave them off, rub the edge or flat of the chocolate bar with your thumb; the heat from your hand should soften the chocolate sufficiently for it to curl without breaking. Store small chocolate curls in the refrigerator or freezer, interleaved with grease-proof paper, until required.

Small chocolate curls are an excellent, last-minute way to decorate a gâteau or mousse, and they are much easier and less messy to make than large curls or caraque. They can be grated directly on to cakes or desserts; they are very easy to make once the technique has been mastered. Chocolate Flavour Cake Covering can also be used to make curls in this way and, with practice, it is possible to produce quite large curls.

CHOCOLATE LEAVES

Any well-defined, well-shaped leaves, free of chemical sprays, can be used for making chocolate leaves, though they must be clean, in perfect condition and bone dry. Using a small paintbrush, paint the underside of the leaves with tempered couverture chocolate (see page 21) or one of the alternatives suggested on page 22, or with melted plain or milk chocolate. Be careful to avoid the chocolate dripping over the edge of the leaf or it will be difficult to peel the leaf off when the chocolate is dry. Leave the leaves on a wire rack in a cool place until set. (If you're in a hurry, put them in the refrigerator or freezer.)

If the chocolate layer on the leaf looks too thin, apply a second coat and leave to set again. If making very large leaves, you may even need to apply a third coat. Carefully peel the leaf away from the chocolate (not the other way round).

To make two-tone chocolate leaves, brush a small amount of white chocolate on to the centre of each leaf first (see above), then cover the remainder of the leaf with plain chocolate. Apply at least two coats.

Handle the chocolate leaves as little as possible as they very easily break in half or, if held for too long, will melt in the heat of your hand. About 225 g (8 oz) chocolate should make 45–50 chocolate rose leaves. Store the leaves in the refrigerator or freezer, interleaved with greaseproof paper, until required.

PIPED CHOCOLATE SHAPES

Draw a series of simple outlines on a piece of greaseproof paper. Turn the paper over. Temper some couverture chocolate (see page 21) or prepare one of the alternatives suggested on page 22, or melt some plain chocolate. Cool the chocolate slightly so that it just coats the back of a spoon and stays there. If it runs off the spoon in a steady stream, it is not ready to use.

Spoon the chocolate into a small paper piping bag. Snip the tip off the bag and pipe the chocolate on to the paper, following the outlines. Allow the chocolate to fall slowly and evenly from the bag; do not try to force the chocolate out or work too quickly. Leave to set, then carefully lift the shapes off the paper with a palette knife. Store in the refrigerator or freezer interleaved with greaseproof paper until required.

Alternatively, pipe the chocolate in an irregular lacy pattern. Instead of marking shapes, drizzle or pipe the chocolate in freehand shapes on to a sheet of greaseproof paper or foil. Leave to set, then peel off the paper.

MODELLING CHOCOLATE

To make your own modelling chocolate, melt 175 g (6 oz) chocolate (milk, plain or white) with 45 ml (3 tbsp) golden syrup or liquid glucose (available from chemists). As soon as the chocolate has melted, remove it from the heat and beat the mixture until it leaves the sides of the bowl clean. Knead briefly and shape into a ball. Cover and chill in the refrigerator for about 30 minutes or until firm.

Roll out the modelling chocolate thinly on a work surface lightly dusted with icing sugar. Cut out shapes as desired. Alternatively, break off small pieces and use like modelling paste to make leaves, flowers and any other 3D shapes you desire. For a two-tone effect, combine white and plain modelling chocolate. To make strips of an even thickness for bows and garlands, or for draping over cakes, run the mixture through a pasta machine set on the thinnest setting.

To make chocolate berries, pull off small pieces of modelling chocolate and roll into small balls the size of cranberries in the palms of your hands. For very special cakes (such as the Chocolate Indulgence Wedding Cake on page 30), cover the berries with tiny pieces of edible gold leaf (available from specialist suppliers, see page 157).

CHOCOLATE HORNS

To make eight chocolate horns, line eight cream horn tins with non-stick baking parchment. Melt 175 g (6 oz) plain, milk or white chocolate (see page 12). Using a pastry brush, brush the inside of the paper with a thick layer of melted chocolate, making sure that it goes right down to the tip. Chill until set.

If necessary, re-melt the remaining chocolate and repeat the coating as above. Carefully remove the chocolate-lined paper from the tins, then peel away the paper (see above). Store in the refrigerator or freezer until required. Serve filled with mousses, fools, sorbets, or ice creams.

To make two-tone chocolate horns, melt 75 g (3 oz) each of plain and white chocolate. Brush half the inside of the paper with white chocolate and leave it to set, then brush the other half with plain chocolate. Repeat the layers if necessary.

CHOCOLATE WAVES

Arrange two or three glass jars or plastic containers on their sides a few inches apart on a baking sheet and secure them with sticky tape. Cut off a 35.5 cm (14 inch) strip of non-stick baking parchment or greaseproof paper and fold it in half lengthways. Spread the paper with a thick layer of melted chocolate and carefully lay it across the jars so that it curves up and down (see above). Freeze for about 5 minutes or until set, then lift the paper off the jars and store in the refrigerator until required. Peel off the paper just before using to decorate cakes, mousses, gâteaux, and wherever a flamboyant chocolate decoration is required. Use a mixture of plain, milk and white chocolate waves for a stunning effect, as on our Death by Chocolate cake (see page 34).

(To make striped waves, simply spread contrasting bands of plain, milk or white chocolate on the paper.)

CHOCOLATE WATTLES

These unusual chocolate decorations reminded us of fencing made from interlaced twigs; hence the name.

Cover a rolling pin with non-stick baking parchment or greaseproof paper, sticking it in place with sticky tape. Temper some couverture chocolate (see page 12) or prepare one of the alternatives suggested on page 22, or melt some plain chocolate. Cool the chocolate slightly so that it just coats the back of a spoon and stays there. If it runs off the spoon in a steady stream, it is not ready to use. Spoon the chocolate into a greaseproof paper piping bag and pipe lines of chocolate backwards and forwards across the paper. Chill or freeze until set, then remove the wattles from the paper and rolling pin and keep in a plastic box, interleaved with greaseproof paper, in the refrigerator until required.

For an extra decorative effect, use wattles made from contrasting colours of chocolate together on the same gâteau or dessert. They look equally stunning dusted with icing sugar or cocoa powder.

TEMPERING CHOCOLATE

The purpose of tempering is to make melted chocolate easier to use, especially for coating, and to produce a good glossy finish. The chocolate is melted, then worked until almost on the point of setting, then reheated to the ideal temperature. Tempered chocolate is not essential for any of the recipes in this book. However, if you want to make chocolate-dipped confectionery and moulded sweets, it is worth the effort. It really does make the chocolate much easier to handle and gives a professional result.

Tempered chocolate will dry rapidly at cool room temperature; it also shrinks slightly as it cools, so it should pull away more easily from a mould. When set, it will have an attractive high gloss finish that will last during storage. Untempered chocolate tends to become dull, streaky or mottled if stored for any length of time.

There are several methods for tempering chocolate. The first step is to melt the chocolate. This can be done in the conventional way as described on page 12 or in a microwave oven, which we found to be the easiest and most convenient.

1 Finely chop about 400 g (14 oz) couverture chocolate and put it in a heatproof bowl. Microwave on HIGH for 2½ minutes or until completely melted. Stir with a wooden spoon; the chocolate should be very viscous. You should be able to see white streaks which look rather like oil on the surface. This is the cocoa butter in the chocolate and it is these particles which the tempering process aims to control. The temperature of the chocolate at this stage should be around 45°C (113°F) (check on a thermometer, but providing the chocolate is fully melted, the temperature is not crucial). Stir the chocolate in the bowl, then tip about three quarters of it on to a marble slab or a clean, dry, cool, smooth work surface. Using a flexible plastic scraper or palette knife, quickly spread the chocolate out on the work surface, using a vigorous paddling or spreading motion to ensure that the chocolate keeps on the move all the time (see right).

2 Once the chocolate is spread as thinly as possible, scrape it up into a pool (see above) and start all over again. Keep repeating this action for about 5 minutes or until the chocolate no longer looks streaky and has cooled to 28°C (82°F). Quickly scrape the chocolate back into the bowl with the remaining melted chocolate and mix the two together thoroughly. The temperature should be 32°C (90°F). Use immediately.

To check if the chocolate is tempered correctly, put a little on the tip of a knife and leave to set. It should set very quickly. If it doesn't set quickly, then it is not tempered, and the only thing to do is start again!

Watchpoints

● Always use couverture chocolate
● Tempering is more difficult on a hot or humid day
● Read the instructions several times so that the method is clear in your mind before you begin
● Cooling to the correct temperature is important
● If the chocolate 'seizes' into a ball on the work surface, this is because the surface was dirty or wet. You will have to start again.
● If you haven't got a microwave, use the conventional method to melt the chocolate. We used the microwave because it is quicker and easier – this becomes especially relevant if more than one attempt at tempering is necessary!

Alternatives to Tempered Chocolate

If you do not want to go to the trouble of tempering, the following alternatives can be used for dipped and moulded chocolates, and for decorations.

1 After tempered couverture, a mixture of couverture and Chocolate Flavour Cake Covering gives the next best result, although the taste and texture is not as good as couverture on its own. This will never set to a crisp 'snap' like tempered couverture.

2 Chocolate Flavour Cake Covering mixed in equal proportions with ordinary chocolate. This will give a thicker coating and it will never set to a crisp 'snap' like tempered couverture.

3 Ordinary chocolate can be mixed with vegetable oil after melting, adding it a teaspoon at a time until it is the desired consistency. Don't add too much or the chocolate will not set hard. Chocolates coated by this method will require chilling in the refrigerator to set. Do not attempt to do this with animal fats or the chocolate will 'seize' (turn into a solid mass).

4 Chocolate Flavour Cake Covering. Use a good quality brand, usually marked 'luxury'.

CHAPTER ONE
CAKES

CHOCOLATE FUDGE CAKE

This gooey, triple-layered chocolate cake is best cut with a large, sharp, wet knife.

MAKES 12–14 SLICES

275 g (10 oz) plain flour
45 ml (3 level tbsp) cocoa powder
6.25 ml (1¼ level tsp) baking powder
2.5 ml (½ level tsp) bicarbonate of soda
a large pinch of salt
125 g (4 oz) plain chocolate
150 g (5 oz) butter, softened
225 g (8 oz) light brown soft sugar
2 eggs, beaten
150 ml (¼ pint) natural yogurt
2.5 ml (½ tsp) vanilla essence

For the fudge icing
450 g (1 lb) icing sugar
125 g (4 oz) cocoa powder
125 g (4 oz) butter
90 ml (6 tbsp) milk

1 Grease three 18 cm (7 inch) sandwich tins, line the bases with greaseproof paper and grease the paper.
2 To make the cake, sift the flour, cocoa powder, baking powder, bicarbonate of soda and salt together.
3 Melt the chocolate (see page 12) and leave to cool slightly.
4 Cream the butter and brown sugar together until pale and fluffy. Gradually beat in the eggs, then fold in the chocolate, the sifted ingredients, yogurt and vanilla essence. Turn the mixture into the prepared tins and level the surfaces.
5 Bake in the oven at 190°C (375°F) mark 5 for 25–30 minutes or until risen and firm to the touch. Turn out on to a wire rack and leave to cool.
6 To make the fudge icing, sift the icing sugar and cocoa powder into a heavy-based

saucepan. Add the butter and the milk, and heat gently until the butter has melted, then beat until the icing is smooth. Remove from the heat.
7 Use some of the fudge icing to sandwich the three cakes together. Cover the sides and top of the cake with the remaining fudge icing. Leave to set.

ENGLISH MADELEINES

Not to be confused with French madeleines, which are baked in shallow, shell-shaped moulds, English madeleines are baked in dariole moulds, then coated in jam and coconut. They're traditionally made with plain sponge, but we thought this chocolate version made a pleasant change.

MAKES 10

125 g (4 oz) butter or margarine, softened
125 g (4 oz) caster sugar
2 eggs, beaten
75 g (3 oz) self-raising flour
25 g (1 oz) cocoa powder
30 ml (2 level tbsp) red jam, sieved
50 g (2 oz) desiccated coconut
chocolate butter cream (see page 152) and chocolate leaves (see page 15), to decorate

1 Grease ten dariole moulds and stand them on a baking sheet.
2 Cream the butter and sugar together until pale and fluffy. Add the eggs, a little at a time, beating well after each addition. Sift the flour and cocoa powder together on to the mixture, then fold in, using a large metal spoon.
3 Turn the mixture into the moulds, filling them three-quarters full. Bake in the oven at 180°C (350°F) mark 4 for about 20 minutes or until well risen and firm to the touch. Turn out on to a wire rack and leave to cool for 20 minutes.

4 When the cakes are almost cold, trim the bases so they stand firmly and are all about the same height. Melt the jam in a saucepan.

5 Spread the coconut out on a large plate. Spear each cake on a skewer, brush with melted jam, then roll in the coconut until evenly coated.

6 Top each madeleine with a small blob of chocolate butter cream and a chocolate leaf.

CHOCOLATE AND APPLE CAKE

This recipe for a Genoese sponge, which is heavy with sweet dessert apples, is made in the classic way. If you are in a hurry, you can cut corners with this particular recipe, because the weight of the apples tends to disguise the texture of the cake! Simply beat the eggs and sugar together with a wooden spoon, then fold in the flour mixture, followed by the melted butter, milk, lemon rind and apples.

SERVES 6

5–10 ml (1–2 tsp) vegetable oil
15–30 ml (1–2 level tbsp) dried breadcrumbs
125 g (4 oz) butter
4 eggs
150 g (5 oz) caster sugar
125 g (4 oz) plain flour
5 ml (1 level tsp) baking powder
a pinch of salt
25 g (1 oz) cocoa powder
finely grated rind of 1 lemon
700 g (1½ lb) Golden Delicious apples, peeled, cored and thinly sliced
icing sugar for dusting

1 Brush the inside of a 23 cm (9 inch) loose-based cake tin with oil. Sprinkle with the breadcrumbs, then shake off the excess.

2 Put the butter in a saucepan and heat gently until melted, then remove from the heat and leave for a few minutes to cool slightly.

3 Put the eggs and sugar in a heatproof bowl standing over a pan of hot water. Whisk until pale and creamy, and thick enough to leave a trail on the surface when the whisk is lifted. Remove from the heat and continue whisking until cool.

4 Sift the flour, baking powder, salt and cocoa powder together into a bowl, then fold half the flour mixture into the egg mixture with a metal spoon.

5 Pour half the cooled butter around the edge of the mixture and fold in very lightly. Gradually fold in the remaining butter and flour alternately. Fold in very lightly or the butter will sink and result in a heavy cake. Fold in the lemon rind and apples. Pour the mixture into the prepared tin.

6 Bake in the oven at 180°C (350°F) mark 4 for about 40 minutes or until a skewer inserted into the centre comes out clean.

7 Leave the cake in the tin for about 5 minutes, then turn out on to a wire rack and leave to cool completely for 2–3 hours. Dust icing sugar over the top of the cake just before serving.

RUM AND CHOCOLATE GUGELHUPF

This famous Austrian cake has as many variations in the spelling of its name as it does in the ingredients included. Basically, it is a rich yeast cake baked in a deep, fluted, ring-shaped mould. This version is a very rich mixture indeed, flavoured with rum, fruit and vanilla and filled with chocolate and poppy seeds. Because the dough is so rich, you need to add extra yeast to make it rise, so don't be tempted to reduce the amount given below.

MAKES ABOUT 20 SLICES

700 g (1½ lb) strong white flour
25 g (1 oz) caster sugar
125 g (4 oz) sultanas
75 g (3 oz) chopped mixed peel
two 7 g sachets fast action dried yeast
300 ml (½ pint) tepid milk
45 ml (3 tbsp) dark rum
5 ml (1 tsp) vanilla essence
2 eggs, beaten
75 g (3 oz) butter, melted

For the filling
50 g (2 oz) poppy seeds
50 g (2 oz) dark brown soft sugar
5 ml (1 level tsp) ground mixed spice
25 g (1 oz) butter
75 g (3 oz) plain chocolate

For the decoration
25 g (1 oz) plain chocolate
25 g (1 oz) white chocolate

1 Put the flour, sugar, sultanas and peel in a bowl and mix together. Sprinkle in the yeast and mix thoroughly. Make a well in the centre, then pour in most of the milk, the rum, vanilla essence, eggs and melted butter. Beat together to make a very soft dough, adding the remaining milk if necessary.

2 Turn the dough on to a lightly floured surface and knead for about 10 minutes or until it is smooth and elastic. Put the dough in an oiled bowl, cover with a clean tea-towel and leave to rise in a warm place for about 1 hour or until doubled in size.

3 Meanwhile, to make the filling, put the poppy seeds, sugar, ground spice and butter in a food processor and purée until smooth. Thoroughly grease a 2.8 litre (5 pint) gugelhupf mould.

4 Turn the dough on to a lightly floured surface and knead again for 5 minutes. Cut off one third of the dough and shape it into a thick sausage. Press this into the base of the mould.

5 Melt the 75 g (3 oz) chocolate (see page 12) and mix it into the filling. Spread over the dough in the mould. Shape the remaining dough into a sausage and put it into the mould on top of the filling. Press it down to seal the pieces of dough together.

6 Cover with a clean tea-towel and leave to rise in a warm place for about 45 minutes or until the dough has risen almost to the top of the mould.

7 Bake in the oven at 190°C (375°F) mark 5 for about 35 minutes or until firm to the touch. Cover with greaseproof paper to prevent it becoming too brown, if necessary. Leave the cake to cool in the tin for about 10 minutes, then carefully turn it out on to a wire rack and leave to cool completely.

8 When the gugelhupf is cold, melt the chocolates in separate bowls and drizzle over the gugelhupf. Leave to set.

DEVIL'S FOOD CAKE

This classic cake comes from the United States. This authentic version makes a cake of huge proportions in true American style!

MAKES 16–18 SLICES

450 g (1 lb) plain flour
15 ml (1 level tbsp) bicarbonate of
soda
a pinch of salt
75 g (3 oz) cocoa powder
345 ml (½ pint, plus 3 tbsp) milk
10 ml (2 tsp) vanilla essence
150 g (5 oz) butter or margarine,
softened
400 g (14 oz) dark brown soft sugar
4 eggs

For the American frosting and
decoration
700 g (1½ lb) caster sugar
3 egg whites
50 g (2 oz) plain chocolate
(optional)

1 Grease three 22 cm (8½ inch) sandwich tins and line the bases with greaseproof paper.

2 To make the cakes, sift the flour, bicarbonate of soda and salt together. Mix the cocoa powder, milk and vanilla essence together until smooth.

3 Using an electric hand-held mixer, cream the butter until pale and fluffy, then gradually beat in the sugar. Add the eggs, one at a time, beating very thoroughly after each addition. Beat in the flour and cocoa mixtures alternately. Divide the mixture between the prepared tins.

4 Bake in the oven at 180°C (350°F) mark 4 for about 35 minutes or until firm to the touch. Turn out on to a wire rack and leave to cool.

5 To make the American frosting, put the sugar and 180 ml (¼ pint, plus 2 tbsp) water in a heavy-based saucepan and heat gently until the sugar has dissolved. When completely dissolved, bring to the boil and boil rapidly to 115°C (240°F). (Use a sugar thermometer to check the temperature.)

6 Meanwhile, put the egg whites in a large deep bowl and whisk until stiff. Slowly pour the hot syrup on to the egg whites, whisking constantly. When all the sugar syrup has been added, continue whisking until the mixture stands in peaks and just starts to become matt around the edges. The icing sets quickly, so work rapidly.

7 Sandwich the three cakes together with a little of the frosting. Spread the remaining frosting over the top and sides of the cake with a palette knife. Pull the icing up into peaks all over. Leave the cake on a wire rack for 30 minutes to allow the icing to set slightly.

8 Melt the chocolate (see page 12), if using, then leave to cool slightly. Spoon it into a greaseproof paper piping bag and drizzle it over the top of the cake. Leave to set completely before cutting.

Opposite: Chocolate Indulgence Wedding Cake (page 30)

CHOCOLATE INDULGENCE WEDDING CAKE

This is a four-tiered chocoholics dream! Once coated with its shiny chocolate icing, the cake can be decorated as desired by the bride-to-be. For an autumn wedding, flowers and leaves in rich russet, gold and brown tones would be perfect. Alternatively, embellish the cake with sheets of gold leaf (see page 17) or tiny white chocolate hearts cut from white chocolate modelling paste (see page 17), using a heart-shaped cutter. Tiny modelling paste balls coated in gold leaf also work well mixed with trailing ivy and flowers.

MAKES 100–120 SLICES

white vegetable fat, for greasing

For the 35.5 cm (14 inch) cake
900 g (2 lb) plain chocolate
900 g (2 lb) unsalted butter, softened
900 g (2 lb) caster sugar
800 g (1¾ lb) ground almonds
20 eggs, separated
350 g (12 oz) fresh brown breadcrumbs
150 ml (10 level tbsp) cocoa powder, sifted
a large pinch of salt

For the 30.5 cm (12 inch) cake
500 g (1 lb 2 oz) plain chocolate
450 g (1 lb) unsalted butter, softened
450 g (1 lb) caster sugar
450 g (1 lb) ground almonds
14 eggs, separated
225 g (8 oz) fresh brown breadcrumbs
120 ml (8 level tbsp) cocoa powder, sifted
a large pinch of salt

For the 25.5 cm (10 inch) cake
275 g (10 oz) plain chocolate
225 g (8 oz) unsalted butter, softened
225 g (8 oz) caster sugar
225 g (8 oz) ground almonds
8 eggs, separated
125 g (4 oz) fresh brown breadcrumbs
60 ml (4 level tbsp) cocoa powder, sifted
a large pinch of salt

For the 20.5 cm (8 inch) cake
225 g (8 oz) plain chocolate
175 g (6 oz) unsalted butter, softened
175 g (6 oz) caster sugar
175 g (6 oz) ground almonds
6 eggs, separated
75 g (3 oz) fresh brown breadcrumbs
45 ml (3 level tbsp) cocoa powder, sifted
a large pinch of salt

For the glaze
550 g (1¼ lb) apricot conserve
90 ml (6 tbsp) liqueur, such as Cointreau or brandy

For the first chocolate icing
900 g (2 lb) couverture or plain chocolate
900 ml (1½ pints) double cream

For the second chocolate icing
450 g (1 lb) couverture or plain chocolate
450 ml (15 fl oz) double cream
45 ml (3 tbsp) liqueur, such as Cointreau or brandy

1 Using white vegetable fat, thoroughly grease the tins and line them with grease-proof paper. Make one cake at a time. Melt the chocolate (see page 12). Using a large mixer, or an electric hand-held whisk, cream together the butter and sugar until pale and fluffy. Stir in the melted chocolate, almonds, egg yolks, breadcrumbs and cocoa powder and beat until well mixed.

2 Using an electric hand-held whisk, whisk the egg whites with the salt until stiff. (When making the larger cakes, it may be necessary to do this in two bowls.) Fold half the egg white into the cake mixture to soften it, then carefully fold in the remainder. Pour into the prepared tin and bake in the oven at 180°C (350°F) mark 4 for about 1¼ hours for the 20.5 cm (8 inch) sponge (this is a slightly deeper cake so it will take longer to cook than the 25.5 cm/10 inch cake), about 1 hour for the 25.5 cm (10 inch) sponge, about 1½ hours for the 30.5 cm (12 inch) sponge, and about 2 hours for the 35.5 cm (14 inch) sponge. When cooked, the cakes should be just firm to the touch.

3 Leave each cake to cool in the tin for about 10 minutes, then carefully turn them out on to a wire rack and leave to cool.

4 Wrap the cakes in greaseproof paper and foil and freeze until required.

5 When ready to assemble, make the apricot glaze. Warm the apricot conserve with the liqueur until it has melted.

6 To make the first layer of chocolate icing, chop or break the chocolate into small pieces. Put it in a heavy-based saucepan with the cream and heat *very gently* until the chocolate has melted, stirring all the time. Remove from the heat and pour into a large bowl. Leave to cool slightly, then beat with a wooden spoon until the mixture is thick enough to spread. (On a hot day it may be necessary to cool it in the refrigerator.)

7 To assemble the cake, unwrap the still-frozen cakes and brush the apricot glaze all over the top and sides of each cake. Spread a thin layer of the icing all over the tops and sides of the cakes, spreading it as smoothly as possible. Leave to set. (This will take about 2 hours – the icing will not set completely but should no longer feel sticky to the touch.) Reserve any leftover icing.

8 Put the largest cake on a cake board, then stack the remaining cakes on top, making sure that they are centred.

9 Stand the stacked cakes on a sturdy icing turntable, if possible, or on a large wire rack or one of the smaller cake tins (upturned). Position the cake in the middle of a large work surface which allows you access to all sides of the cake if you're not using a turntable. Make up a second batch of chocolate icing using any leftover icing with the chocolate, cream and liqueur for the second icing. Remove from the heat and cool very slightly or until just thick enough to coat the back of a spoon.

10 Pour the icing into a measuring jug, then pour it in a steady flow on to the top cake, allowing it to run all the way down to the bottom tier. If using a turntable, turn the cake round after pouring the first jugful to ensure that the coating is even. If not using a turntable, walk round the cake to do this, rather than attempting to turn the cake. The icing will run on to the cake board; make sure that this, too, is covered evenly. Try to avoid spreading the icing with a palette knife because this will dull the shine. Leave to set completely before moving.

11 When the icing has set, tie a ribbon around the sides of the board and secure with pins. Carefully position it on a cake stand or a second cake board. The cake can be kept like this for 2 days, although in the summer or when the weather is humid the icing will spoil if kept for more than a day. Add the final decoration of chocolate modelling paste balls or hearts, or gold leaf or chocolate leaves, or caraque, the morning of the wedding.

12 To serve the cake, lift the cakes off one tier at a time, using palette knives. Cut into thin slices with a large, sharp knife.

WHITE CHOCOLATE WEDDING CAKE

This is a spectacular three-tiered concoction of light sponges with a rich gooey chocolate mousse filling covered in cream and masses of white chocolate curls. You will need three large round cake tins measuring 35.5 cm (14 inches), 28 cm (11 inches) and 20.5 cm (8 inches). To assemble the cake, you will need two pieces of thick cardboard the same diameter as the middle and top cakes, and about 16 wooden chopsticks. Decorate the cake with fresh flowers to complement the bride's bouquet. Make the all-important white chocolate curls in advance and store in the refrigerator or freezer. The undecorated cakes freeze well and will thaw out overnight at room temperature. They can be decorated the night before the wedding and stored in a cool place (it doesn't have to be the refrigerator) overnight. It is easiest and safest to make and bake one sponge at a time. Do not attempt this recipe if you don't own an electric whisk. A very large bowl is also necessary, especially for the largest cake. To make a smaller version, omit the bottom cake and make just the middle and top layers as below.

MAKES 60–80 SLICES

white vegetable fat, for greasing

For the 35.5 cm (14 inch) cake
200 g (7 oz) butter
14 eggs
400 g (14 oz) caster sugar
275 g (10 oz) plain flour
125 g (4 oz) cornflour

For the 28 cm (11 inch) cake
125 g (4 oz) butter
8 eggs
225 g (8 oz) caster sugar
200 g (7 oz) plain flour
25 g (1 oz) cornflour

For the 20.5 cm (8 inch) cake
75 g (3 oz) butter
6 eggs
175 g (6 oz) caster sugar
150 g (5 oz) plain flour
25 g (1 oz) cornflour

For the mousse filling
700 g (1½ lb) plain chocolate
120 ml (8 tbsp) brandy
8 eggs, separated
1.1 litres (2 pints) double cream
2 sachets (20 ml/4 level tsp)
powdered gelatine

For the decoration
1.1 litres (2 pints) double cream
white chocolate curls made with
1.1 kg (2½ lb) chocolate
(see page 13)
icing sugar
fresh flowers

1 Grease the tins (see recipe introduction) thoroughly using white vegetable fat and line with greaseproof paper.
2 Make one cake at a time. Put the butter into a saucepan and heat gently until melted, then remove from the heat and leave to stand for a few minutes to cool slightly.
3 Put the eggs and sugar in a large bowl, place over a saucepan of hot water and whisk with an electric hand-held whisk until very pale and creamy and thick enough to leave a trail on the surface when the whisk is lifted. As an approximate guide, the large cake should be whisked for 25–30 minutes, the medium cake for 15 minutes and the small cake for about 10 minutes. Remove the mixture from the heat and continue whisking until cool.
4 Sift the flours together into a bowl. Fold half of the flour into the egg mixture with a metal spoon. Pour half the cooled butter around the edge of the mixture and fold in

very lightly and carefully or the butter will sink and the result will be a heavy cake. Gradually fold in the remaining flour and butter as before.

5 Pour the mixture into the prepared tin. Bake in the oven at 180°C (350°F) mark 4 for 1–1¼ hours for the largest cake, 40–45 minutes for the middle cake and 30–35 minutes for the smallest cake. When cooked, each cake should be well risen, firm to the touch and just shrinking away from the sides of the tin. Turn out on to a wire rack and leave to cool. Wrap and store in the freezer, if necessary, until ready to assemble.

6 To make the mousse, melt the chocolate (see page 12), then remove from the heat and stir in the brandy and egg yolks. Whip the cream until it just stands in soft peaks, then fold it into the chocolate mixture.

7 In a small heatproof bowl, sprinkle the gelatine on to 60 ml (4 tbsp) water. Stand the bowl over a pan of simmering water and stir until the gelatine has dissolved. Cool, then stir into the chocolate mixture. Whisk the egg whites until stiff, then fold in.

8 Cut each cake horizontally in half. Put the bottom half of each cake back into the base of each tin. Pour the mousse on top, dividing it proportionally between each tin. Chill until set. Put the second half of each

sponge back into its tin on top of the mousse, and press together. Carefully turn the cakes out.

9 For the decoration, whip the cream until it just holds its shape. Put the largest cake on to a cake board and cover with a thin layer of cream. Place the middle cake on a round of stiff cardboard (see introduction).

10 Push a wooden chopstick into the middle of the bottom layer of cake. With a pen, mark the stick about 2.5 cm (1 inch) above the top of the cake. Pull it out and cut it off with a Stanley knife, using the mark as a guide. Cut seven more chopsticks to the same height.

11 Insert the chopsticks in a circle into the bottom cake. Stand the middle cake on top to check that it stands level. Remove the cake, then repeat the procedure with the middle and top sponges, cutting eight more chopsticks to the required height.

12 Cover the middle and top cakes with whipped cream (do this on a board, not with the cakes in position). Cover all the cakes completely with the chocolate curls and dredge with icing sugar.

13 Assemble the cake where it is to be served. (Do not attempt to move the cake once the tiers are in position!) Stack the cakes, one on top of another, and decorate with fresh flowers as desired.

DEATH BY CHOCOLATE

MAKES 24 SLICES

225 g (8 oz) plain chocolate
125 g (4 oz) butter
350 g (12 oz) caster sugar
2.5 ml (½ tsp) vanilla essence
2 eggs, separated
150 ml (¼ pint) soured cream
350 g (12 oz) self-raising flour
5 ml (1 level tsp) bicarbonate of
soda

For the filling
450 g (1 lb) couverture or plain
chocolate
225 g (8 oz) butter
90 ml (6 tbsp) brandy
350 g (12 oz) white chocolate

For the icing and decoration
200 g (7 oz) couverture or plain
chocolate, finely chopped
200 ml (7 fl oz) double cream
plain, milk and white chocolate
waves (see page 19)

1 Grease a 25.5 cm (10 inch) spring-release cake tin and line the base with greaseproof paper.

2 To make the cake, melt the chocolate with the butter and 150 ml (¼ pint) water (see page 12). Beat in the sugar and vanilla essence, then leave to cool.

3 Beat the egg yolks into the cooled chocolate mixture, then fold in the soured cream, flour and bicarbonate of soda. Whisk the egg whites until stiff, then fold into the mixture. Pour the mixture into the prepared tin.

4 Bake in the oven at 180°C (350°F) mark 4 for about 1 hour or until well risen and slightly shrinking away from the sides of the tin. (The cake will have a slight crust.) Turn the cake out on to a wire rack to cool.

5 To make the filling, melt the couverture or plain chocolate with the butter. Stir in 60 ml (4 tbsp) of the brandy and leave until thick enough to spread.

6 Cut the cake horizontally into three even layers. Don't worry if the middle layer has a hole in it (this will happen if the cake has sunk slightly); the hole will not show once the cake is assembled. Sprinkle the cut sides with the remaining brandy. Melt the white chocolate and spread it thinly over the three layers of sponge. Leave to set.

7 To assemble the cake, put the bottom layer back in the tin, white chocolate side up. Spread with half of the filling, top with a second layer of sponge, white chocolate side uppermost, and spread with the remaining filling. Put the final layer of sponge on top, white chocolate side down. Cover and chill until set.

8 Carefully remove the cake from the tin and ease off the base. Run a palette knife around the sides to make them smooth, if necessary. Stand the cake on a wire rack placed over a baking sheet.

9 To make the icing, put the chocolate in a large heatproof bowl. Put the cream in a heavy-based saucepan and bring to the boil. (Watch it carefully because it will boil over once it reaches boiling point.) As soon as it reaches boiling point, pour it over the chocolate. Leave for about 5 minutes, undisturbed, then whisk the mixture with a balloon whisk, starting slowly from the centre of the bowl and gradually whisking more vigorously. The icing should be perfectly smooth and glossy.

10 Pour the icing over the cake, letting it run down the sides and using a palette knife to help if necessary. Leave to set (not in the refrigerator or the icing will be spoilt). When the icing has set, decorate with chocolate waves.

CINNAMON CHOCOLATE TORTE

MAKES 6–8 SLICES

175 g (6 oz) plain chocolate
175 g (6 oz) butter, softened
200 g (7 oz) caster sugar
5 eggs, separated
150 g (5 oz) plain flour
*10 ml (2 level tsp) ground
cinnamon*
75 g (3 oz) ground almonds
icing sugar for dusting

For the filling
90 ml (6 tbsp) apricot jam
30 ml (2 tbsp) lemon juice
5 ml (1 level tsp) ground cinnamon
300 ml (½ pint) whipping cream

1 Grease and line two 19 cm (7½ inch) sandwich tins.
2 To make the cake, melt the chocolate (see page 12) and leave to cool slightly.
3 Cream the butter and sugar together until pale and fluffy. Beat in the egg yolks, then add the melted chocolate with 45 ml (3 tbsp) water, mixing well.
4 Whisk the egg whites until they stand in soft peaks. Sift the flour with the cinnamon and fold into the creamed mixture with the ground almonds and egg whites. Spoon the mixture into the prepared tins.
5 Bake in the oven at 190°C (375°F) mark 5 for 35–40 minutes or until a skewer inserted into the centre comes out clean. Turn the cakes out on to a wire rack and leave to cool. Cut each cake horizontally into two layers.
6 To make the filling, melt the apricot jam with the lemon juice and cinnamon. Leave to cool. Whip the cream until stiff. Spread the apricot mixture on the cake layers and sandwich them together with the whipped cream. Dust the top with icing sugar just before serving.

CHOCOLATE WALNUT LOAF

If wrapped in foil and stored in an airtight container, this loaf will keep for 4 days.

MAKES 12–14 SLICES

*150 g (5 oz) dried stoned dates,
roughly chopped*
150 g (5 oz) plain chocolate
40 g (1½ oz) butter or margarine
225 g (8 oz) plain flour
40 g (1½ oz) caster sugar
5 ml (1 level tsp) salt
5 ml (1 level tsp) baking powder
*5 ml (1 level tsp) bicarbonate of
soda*
1 egg
about 150 ml (¼ pint) milk
5 ml (1 tsp) vanilla essence
*150 g (5 oz) walnut pieces, roughly
chopped*
30 ml (2 level tbsp) demerara sugar

1 Lightly grease a 900 g (2 lb), 1.1–1.3 litre (2–2¼ pint) loaf tin and line the base with greaseproof paper.
2 Put the dates in a small bowl. Pour over 150 ml (¼ pint) boiling water and leave to stand for 30 minutes. Melt the chocolate with the butter (see page 12).
3 Mix together the flour, caster sugar, salt, baking powder and bicarbonate of soda.
4 Whisk together the egg, milk and vanilla essence. Beat into the dry ingredients with all but 30 ml (2 level tbsp) of the walnuts, the dates and soaking liquor, and the melted chocolate. Spoon the mixture into the prepared tin and level the surface. Sprinkle over the reserved walnuts and the demerara sugar.
5 Bake at 180°C (350°F) mark 4 for about 1¼ hours or until a skewer inserted in the centre comes out clean. Cool in the tin for 10 minutes before turning out on to a wire rack to cool completely.

BATTENBURG CAKE

MAKES ABOUT 10 SLICES

175 g (6 oz) butter or margarine,
softened
175 g (6 oz) caster sugar
a few drops of vanilla essence
3 eggs, beaten
175 g (6 oz) self-raising flour
15 g (½ oz) cocoa powder, sifted
milk
apricot jam or orange cheese
350 g (12 oz) white marzipan or
almond paste

1 Grease and line a Swiss roll tin measuring 30.5×20.5×2 cm (12×8×¾ inch) and divide it lengthways with a 'wall' of greaseproof paper or kitchen foil.

2 Cream the butter and sugar together until pale and fluffy. Add the vanilla essence, then add the eggs, a little at a time, beating well after each addition. When all the egg has been added, lightly fold in the flour.

3 Turn half of the mixture into one side of the tin. Fold the cocoa powder into the other half with a little milk and spoon this mixture into the second side of the tin.

4 Bake in the oven at 190°C (375°F) mark 5 for 40–45 minutes or until well risen and firm to the touch. Turn out on to a wire rack and leave to cool.

5 When the cake is cold, cut each half in half lengthways. Spread all the sides of the strips with apricot jam or orange cheese and stick each plain strip to a brown strip. Then stick one double strip on top of the other, so that the colours alternate. Press the pieces together well.

6 Roll out the marzipan thinly on a work surface dusted with a little icing sugar, into a rectangle measuring about 35.5×25.5 cm (14×10 inches). Wrap completely around the cake. Press firmly against the sides and trim the edges. Crimp along the outer edges and score the top of the cake with a sharp knife to make a decorative criss-cross pattern in the marzipan.

Overleaf: Battenburg Cake

CAPPUCCINO CAKE

This dark chocolate and coffee cake has a frothy cream and cocoa topping, reminiscent of a good cappuccino.

MAKES 16–18 SLICES

225 g (8 oz) plain chocolate
15 ml (1 level tbsp) instant coffee
granules
225 g (8 oz) butter or margarine,
softened
225 g (8 oz) dark brown soft sugar
5 eggs
125 g (4 oz) ground almonds
125 g (4 oz) cornflour

To finish
30 ml (2 tbsp) strong coffee, cooled
30 ml (2 tbsp) dark rum
300 ml (½ pint) whipping cream
cocoa powder, to decorate

1 Grease a 23 cm (9 inch) round spring-release cake tin and line the base with greaseproof paper.

2 To make the cake, melt the chocolate with the instant coffee (see page 12) and leave to cool slightly.

3 Cream the butter and sugar together until pale and fluffy. Beat in the eggs, one at a time, beating well after each addition. Fold in the almonds, cornflour and melted chocolate. Pour the mixture into the prepared tin and level the surface.

4 Bake in the oven at 180°C (350°F) mark 4 for about 1¼ hours or until risen and just firm to the touch. Cover the cake with greaseproof paper to prevent it becoming too brown, if necessary. Leave the cake to cool in the tin.

5 When the cake is cold, prick it all over with a fine skewer. Mix the coffee and rum together, and pour evenly over the cake. Leave for at least 30 minutes.

6 Whip the cream until it just holds its shape. Remove the cake from the tin and transfer it to a serving plate. Spoon the cream on top and spread it evenly with a palette knife. Sift a little cocoa powder over the cream.

EGGLESS CHOCOLATE CAKE

This cake was created in response to requests for a cake made without eggs, suitable for vegans or those with an egg allergy. No one will ever guess that there's anything unusual about it! It's really moist, chocolatey and irresistible. It also keeps very well, wrapped in foil or in an airtight tin.

MAKES ABOUT 12 SLICES

125 g (4 oz) creamed coconut
50 g (2 oz) cocoa powder
400 g (14 oz) self-raising flour
5 ml (1 level tsp) baking powder
a large pinch of salt
225 g (8 oz) light brown soft sugar
200 ml (7 fl oz) sunflower oil
icing sugar for dusting (optional)

1 Oil and line a 1.7 litre (3 pint) loaf tin.

2 Pour 650 ml (22 fl oz) boiling water over the coconut and stir until it dissolves. Leave to cool for 30 minutes.

3 Sift the cocoa powder, flour, baking powder and salt into a bowl and mix together with the sugar. Make a well in the centre, then pour in the coconut mixture and the oil. Beat the ingredients together thoroughly to make a smooth, thick batter.

4 Pour into the prepared tin and bake in the oven at 180°C (350°F) mark 4 for 1¼ hours or until well risen and just firm to the touch. Leave to cool in the tin for 10 minutes, then turn out on to a wire rack and leave to cool completely. Dust with icing sugar before serving, if liked.

CHOCOLATE CRACKLES

MAKES 12

*225 g (8 oz) plain or milk
chocolate, broken into pieces
15 ml (1 tbsp) golden syrup
50 g (2 oz) butter or margarine
50 g (2 oz) Corn Flakes or Rice
Krispies*

1 Place 12 paper cases on a baking sheet.
2 Melt the chocolate in a saucepan with the syrup and butter. Fold in the Corn Flakes or Rice Krispies, mix well, and divide between the cases. Chill in the refrigerator.

CHOCOLATE NUT MUFFINS

These are particularly good served warm, fresh from the oven.

MAKES 12

*125 g (4 oz) plain chocolate
125 g (4 oz) shelled Brazil nuts,
roughly chopped
225 g (8 oz) self-raising flour
5 ml (1 level tsp) baking powder
50 g (2 oz) dark brown soft sugar
225 ml (8 fl oz) milk
60 ml (4 tbsp) sunflower oil
5 ml (1 tsp) vanilla essence
1 egg (size 1)*

1 Place 12 large paper cases in 12 deep muffin tins (see Note).
2 Melt the chocolate (see page 12), then remove from the heat and beat in all the remaining ingredients.
3 Spoon the mixture into the paper cases and bake in the oven at 220°C (425°F) mark 7 for 15–20 minutes or until well risen and firm to the touch.

DOUBLE CHOCOLATE MUFFINS

MAKES 12

*125 g (4 oz) plain chocolate
50 g (2 oz) cocoa powder
225 g (8 oz) self-raising flour
5 ml (1 level tsp) baking powder
50 g (2 oz) dark brown soft sugar
a pinch of salt
125 g (4 oz) plain chocolate drops
225 ml (8 fl oz) milk
60 ml (4 tbsp) vegetable oil
5 ml (1 tsp) vanilla essence
1 egg*

1 Place 12 large paper cases in 12 deep muffin tins (see Note).
2 Melt the plain chocolate (see page 12). Remove from the heat and stir in the remaining ingredients. Beat thoroughly together.
3 Spoon the mixture into the paper cases and bake in the oven at 220°C (425°F) mark 7 for 15 minutes or until well risen and firm to the touch. Serve warm.

Note
The recipes on this page are for American-style muffins. They should be made in proper deep muffin tins – ordinary bun tins are too shallow.

EXCEEDINGLY GOOEY CHOCOLATE BROWNIES

As the name suggests, this makes very rich, gooey brownies. Serve as a dessert with ice cream or chilled yogurt.

MAKES 24

550 g (1¼ lb) plain chocolate
225 g (8 oz) butter
3 eggs
30 ml (2 tbsp) freshly made strong coffee
225 g (8 oz) caster sugar
75 g (3 oz) self-raising flour
2.5 ml (½ level tsp) salt
175 g (6 oz) walnut halves, chopped
5 ml (1 tsp) vanilla essence

1 Grease and line a baking tin measuring 22×29.5 cm (8½×11½ inches) across the top and 19×26.5 cm (7½×10½ inches) across the base.
2 Using a very sharp knife, roughly chop 225 g (8 oz) of the chocolate and set aside. Melt the remaining chocolate with the butter (see page 12) and leave to cool slightly.
3 Mix the eggs, coffee and sugar together in a large bowl, then gradually beat in the melted chocolate. Fold in the flour, salt, walnuts, vanilla essence and chopped chocolate, and pour into the prepared tin.
4 Bake in the oven at 190°C (375°F) mark 5 for 45 minutes or until *just* firm to the touch in the centre. Do not overcook or the soft, gooey texture will be ruined. Leave to cool in the tin.
5 When the cake is completely cold, turn it out on to a board and trim the edges. Cut into 24 squares.

CHOCOLATE CUP CAKES

MAKES 12–14

125 g (4 oz) butter or margarine, softened
125 g (4 oz) light brown soft sugar
50 g (2 oz) self-raising wholemeal flour
25 g (1 oz) self-raising white flour
25 g (1 oz) cocoa powder, sifted
a pinch of baking powder
2 eggs

For the chocolate fudgy topping
75 g (3 oz) plain chocolate
25 g (1 oz) butter or margarine
75 g (3 oz) icing sugar, sifted

1 Spread 12–14 paper cases out on a baking sheet or put them into patty tins.
2 Put the butter, sugar, flours, cocoa powder, baking powder and eggs in a food processor and process until smooth. Fill the paper cases two-thirds full with the mixture.
3 Bake in the oven at 190°C (375°F) mark 5 for 15 minutes or until well risen and firm to the touch. Transfer to a wire rack and leave to cool.
4 To make the topping, melt the chocolate with the butter (see page 12). Remove from the heat. Add the icing sugar and 30 ml (2 tbsp) warm water and beat well.
5 Spread the chocolate icing over the cup cakes, working quickly before it begins to set. Leave to set.

Preceding page: Exceedingly Gooey Chocolate Brownies

WHISKED SPONGE

This classic fatless sponge does not keep well and should be eaten on the day it is made.

MAKES ABOUT 8 SLICES

3 eggs
75 g (3 oz) caster sugar
75 g (3 oz) less 15 ml (1 level tbsp)
plain flour
15 ml (1 level tbsp) cocoa powder
whipped cream, to fill
icing sugar, to dredge

1 Grease two 18 cm (7 inch) sandwich tins, line the bases with greaseproof paper and grease the paper. Dust the insides of the tins with a mixture of flour and caster sugar.
2 Put the eggs and sugar in a large heat-proof bowl and stand it over a saucepan of hot water. Whisk the eggs and sugar until doubled in volume and thick enough to leave a thin trail on the surface of the mixture when the whisk is lifted.
3 Remove the bowl from the heat and continue whisking for a further 5 minutes or until the mixture is cool.
4 Sift together the flour and cocoa powder. Sift half over the egg mixture and fold it in very lightly, using a large metal spoon. Sift and fold in the remaining flour and cocoa in the same way.
5 Pour the mixture into the prepared tins, tilting the tins to spread the mixture evenly. Do not use a palette knife or spatula to smooth the mixture as this will crush out the air bubbles.
6 Bake in the oven at 190°C (375°F) mark 5 for 20–25 minutes or until well risen, firm to the touch and beginning to shrink away from the sides of the tins. Turn out on to a wire rack and leave to cool.
7 When the cakes are cold, sandwich them together with cream and dredge the top with icing sugar.

Variation

Chocolate Swiss Roll Make the Whisked Sponge mixture as directed but use 152 g (4 oz) less 25 ml (1½ level tbsp) plain flour and 25 ml (1½ level tbsp) cocoa powder and fold it in with 15 ml (1 tbsp) hot water. Pour the mixture into a lined 33 × 23 cm (13 × 9 inch) Swiss roll tin.

1 Tilt the tin backwards and forwards to spread the mixture in an even layer. Bake in the oven at 200°C (400°F) mark 6 for about 10 minutes or until pale golden brown and well risen.
2 Meanwhile, place a sheet of greaseproof paper on top of a damp tea-towel. Dredge the paper with caster sugar.
3 Quickly turn the cake out on to the paper, trim off the crusty edges and spread with Chocolate Butter Cream (see page 152) or whipped cream. Roll up the cake with the aid of the paper. Make the first turn firmly so that the whole cake will roll evenly and have a good shape when finished, but continue rolling more lightly.
4 Place the Swiss roll, seam-side down, on a wire rack and dredge with icing sugar.

BÛCHE DE NOËL

Bûche de Noël is traditionally eaten in France at Christmas time. This and the English Yule Log date back to the days when a huge log used to be burnt on Christmas Eve.

MAKES ABOUT **8** SLICES

3 eggs
125 g (4 oz) caster sugar
75 g (3 oz) plain flour
30 ml (2 level tbsp) cocoa powder
440 g (15½ oz) can sweetened
chestnut purée

For the butter cream
225 g (8 oz) unsalted butter,
softened
50 g (2 oz) plain chocolate
450 g (1 lb) icing sugar

For the meringue mushrooms
1 egg white
50 g (2 oz) caster sugar

For the decoration
holly sprigs
icing sugar for dusting

1 To make the meringue mushrooms, line a baking sheet with non-stick baking parchment. Whisk the egg white until stiff, add half of the sugar and whisk again until stiff. Fold in the remaining sugar.

2 Spoon the meringue into a piping bag fitted with a plain nozzle. Pipe the meringue on to the prepared baking sheet to resemble small mushroom caps and, separately, mushroom stalks. Bake in the oven at 110°C (225°F) mark ¼ for about 1½ hours or until dry. Cool for at least 15 minutes.

3 To make the cake, grease a 33×23 cm (13×9 inch) Swiss roll tin. Line with greaseproof paper and grease the paper. Dredge with a little caster sugar, then with a little flour, knocking out any excess.

4 Put the eggs and sugar in a deep heat-proof bowl and stand it over a saucepan of simmering water. Whisk until thick enough to leave a trail on the surface when the whisk is lifted. Do not overheat the mixture by letting the bowl come into contact with the simmering water or by having the heat under the saucepan too high.

5 Take the bowl off the saucepan and continue whisking the mixture for 5 minutes or until cool. Sift in the flour and cocoa and gently fold into the mixture. Fold in 15 ml (1 tbsp) hot water.

6 Pour the mixture gently into the prepared tin and lightly level the surface. Bake in the oven at 200°C (400°F) mark 6 for about 10 minutes or until slightly shrunk away from the sides of the tin.

7 Meanwhile, place a sheet of greaseproof paper on top of a tea-towel. Dredge the paper with caster sugar and turn the cake out on to it. Trim off the crusty edges with a sharp knife. Roll up the cake with the paper inside. Transfer to a wire rack, seam side down, and leave to cool for 20 minutes.

8 To make the butter cream, beat the butter until soft. Melt the chocolate with 15 ml (1 tbsp) water (see page 12), then leave to cool slightly. Gradually sift and beat the icing sugar into the softened butter, then add the melted chocolate.

9 Unroll the cold Swiss roll and spread the chestnut purée over the surface. Roll up again without the paper inside. Place on a cake board or plate.

10 Cut a thick diagonal slice off one end of the Swiss roll and attach with butter cream to the side of the roll.

11 Using a piping bag and a large star nozzle, pipe thin lines of butter cream over the log. Pipe one or two swirls of butter cream to represent knots in the wood. Stick the meringue caps on top of the stalks with a little butter cream to form mushrooms. Decorate the log with the mushrooms and sprigs of holly. Dust lightly with icing sugar.

CHAPTER TWO

GÂTEAUX
AND
MERINGUES

SQUIDGY CHOCOLATE MOUSSE CAKE

This delicious combination of a rich chocolate sponge topped with soft, squidgy chocolate mousse is perfect for a dinner-party dessert.

SERVES 8

225 g (8 oz) plain chocolate
15 ml (1 tbsp) orange-flavoured liqueur
5 eggs, separated
150 g (5 oz) caster sugar
125 g (4 oz) unsalted butter, softened

For the mousse
225 g (8 oz) plain chocolate
30 ml (2 tbsp) orange-flavoured liqueur
4 eggs, separated

For the decoration
blanched julienne strips of orange rind
grated chocolate

1 Grease a 20.5 cm (8 inch) spring-release cake tin, line with greaseproof paper and grease the paper.

2 Melt the chocolate (see page 12), stir in the orange-flavoured liqueur and leave to cool slightly.

3 Meanwhile, using an electric whisk, whisk the five egg yolks and the sugar together in a heatproof bowl standing over a saucepan of hot water until thick and creamy. Beat in the butter, a little at a time, until smooth, then beat in the chocolate.

4 Whisk the five egg whites until stiff, then fold into the chocolate mixture. Turn into the prepared tin.

5 Bake in the oven at 180°C (350°F) mark 4 for 40 minutes or until risen and firm. Leave the cake to cool in the tin for 1 hour.

6 To make the mousse layer, melt the chocolate, then stir in the liqueur. Remove from the heat and leave to cool for 1–2 minutes. Beat the egg yolks into the chocolate mixture. Whisk the egg whites until stiff, then fold into the chocolate mixture.

7 Press the crust down on the baked cake with your fingers and pour the mousse mixture over it. Chill overnight.

8 The next day, remove the cake carefully from the tin and put it on a serving plate. Arrange strips of orange rind around the outside edge and decorate with grated chocolate. Keep in the refrigerator until about 30 minutes before serving.

BLACK FOREST GÂTEAU

This famous and much-loved cake is from Germany. The cherries should really be fresh morello cherries, but as these are not always easy to come by, we've used canned cherries instead. When fresh morello cherries are available, poach them in a sugar syrup and carefully remove their stones before using them in the gâteau.

SERVES 10

75 g (3 oz) butter
6 eggs
175 g (6 oz) caster sugar
125 g (4 oz) plain flour
50 g (2 oz) cocoa powder
2.5 ml (½ tsp) vanilla essence

For the filling and decoration
two 425 g (15 oz) cans stoned black
cherries, drained and syrup reserved
60 ml (4 tbsp) kirsch
600 ml (1 pint) whipping cream
125 g (4 oz) chocolate caraque
(see page 13)
5 ml (1 level tsp) arrowroot

1 Grease a deep 23 cm (9 inch) round cake tin and line the base with greaseproof paper.
2 To make the cake, put the butter in a heatproof bowl, place it over a saucepan of warm water and beat until really soft but not melted.
3 Using an electric hand-held whisk, whisk the eggs and sugar together in a large heatproof bowl standing over a pan of simmering water until pale and creamy, and thick enough to leave a trail on the surface when the whisk is lifted. Remove from the heat and continue whisking until cool.
4 Sift the flour and cocoa powder together,

then lightly fold into the mixture with a metal spoon. Fold in the vanilla essence and softened butter. Turn the mixture into the prepared tin and tilt the tin to spread the mixture evenly.
5 Bake in the oven at 180°C (350°F) mark 4 for about 40 minutes or until well risen, firm to the touch and beginning to shrink away from the sides of the tin. Turn the cake out of the tin on to a piece of greaseproof paper on a wire rack and leave to cool for 30 minutes. Cut the cake horizontally into three layers.
6 Place one layer on a flat plate. To make the filling, mix together 75 ml (5 tbsp) of the cherry syrup and the kirsch. Spoon 45 ml (3 tbsp) over the cake layer.
7 Whip the cream until it just holds its shape, then spread a little in a thin layer over the soaked sponge. Reserve a quarter of the cherries for decoration and scatter half the remainder over the cream.
8 Repeat the layers of sponge, syrup, cream and cherries. Top with the third cake round and spoon over the remaining kirsch-flavoured syrup.
9 Reserve one third of the remaining cream for decoration and spread the remainder in a thin layer around the sides of the cake. Press on the chocolate caraque, reserving a little to decorate the top.
10 Spoon the remaining cream into a piping bag fitted with a large star nozzle and pipe whirls of cream around the top edge of the cake. Top each whirl with a piece of chocolate caraque.
11 Fill the centre with the reserved cherries. Blend the arrowroot with 45 ml (3 tbsp) cherry syrup in a small saucepan. Bring to the boil and boil, stirring, for a few minutes or until the mixture is clear. Brush the glaze over the cherries.

RIGO JACSI

Absolute temptation! These rich squares of chocolate gâteau, classic in their make-up of chocolate flavoured Genoese and ganache, were named after a gypsy violinist, who was said to have broken the heart of many a princess.

MAKES 12 SQUARES

*½ quantity chocolate genoese mixture
(see page 52)*

For the Chocolate Ganache
*425 g (15 oz) plain chocolate
600 ml (1 pint) double cream
45 ml (3 tbsp) brandy*

For the icing
*125 g (4 oz) plain chocolate
30 ml (2 tbsp) brandy
125 g (4 oz) icing sugar, sifted*

For the spun sugar (optional)
*125 g (4 oz) granulated sugar
about 30 ml (2 level tbsp) liquid
glucose*

1 Grease a 23 × 33 cm (9 × 13 inch) Swiss roll tin and line the base with greaseproof paper. Make up the cake mixture as described on page 52 and spread it evenly in the prepared tin.

2 Bake in the oven at 180°C (350°F) mark 4 for 20–25 minutes or until well risen, firm to the touch and beginning to shrink away from the sides of the tin. Cool in the tin.

3 To make the ganache, break the chocolate into small pieces. Place the chocolate and cream in a large saucepan and heat gently, stirring, until the chocolate melts and blends with the cream. Do not boil.

4 Pour the ganache into a bowl and leave to cool, but not set hard, stirring frequently to prevent a skin forming. When cold, whip the ganache with the brandy until very light and fluffy, taking care not to overwhip the mixture.

5 Cut the chocolate sponge across into two pieces. Place one piece in a deep square cake tin, placing it against two sides of the tin, then form a false 'wall' for the other side, with several thicknesses of foil.

6 Spoon the whipped ganache on top of the sponge in the tin and spread evenly to a depth of about 5 cm (2 inches). Place the second layer of sponge on top. Chill for at least 1 hour.

7 To make the icing, break the chocolate into small pieces. Place in a small saucepan with 15 ml (1 tbsp) water, the brandy and icing sugar. Stir over a gentle heat until the chocolate melts and blends with the icing sugar to make a smooth icing. Spread the icing over the top layer and leave to set.

8 Carefully remove the 'wall' from around the cake. Cut the gâteau into 12 pieces, using a sharp knife dipped in hot water and dried each time before cutting. Chill until 20–30 minutes before serving.

9 To make the spun sugar, if using, cover a rolling pin with foil and oil it lightly. Have ready two forks tied or taped together back to back.

10 Put the sugar and 50 ml (2 fl oz) water in a small heavy-based saucepan and heat gently until melted. Bring to the boil, then add the glucose. Half cover the pan and boil to 152°C (305°F). Immediately dip the base of the pan into cold water and cool for 30 seconds only.

11 Dip the prongs of the forks in the syrup and, holding the covered rolling pin in the other hand, flick the forks backwards and forwards over the rolling pin to form long strands of sugar. Repeat with the remaining syrup, then place on an oiled baking sheet. Use to decorate the gâteau just before serving.

CHOCOLATE AND CHESTNUT GÂTEAU

For this stunning gâteau, thin layers of chocolate sponge are sandwiched together with a rich, gooey chestnut cream. The easiest way to cut the cake horizontally into four is to lay the cake flat on a board, then to slice through it using a large knife with a long, sharp blade. When sandwiching the layers back together, make sure they are replaced in their original position, or you may end up with a lopsided cake.

SERVES 12

For the chocolate genoese
75 g (3 oz) butter
6 eggs
175 g (6 oz) caster sugar
125 g (4 oz) plain flour
30 ml (2 level tbsp) cornflour
25 g (1 oz) cocoa powder

For the filling and decoration
125 g (4 oz) plain chocolate
425 g (15 oz) can unsweetened chestnut purée
300 ml (½ pint) double cream
30 ml (2 tbsp) brandy
canned whole chestnuts, drained
grated chocolate
icing sugar for dusting

1 Grease a 23 cm (9 inch) spring-release cake tin and line with greaseproof paper.
2 Melt the butter, then remove from the heat and leave to cool slightly.

3 Put the eggs and sugar in a heatproof bowl standing over a saucepan of hot water. Using an electric hand-held whisk, whisk the eggs and sugar together until pale and creamy, and thick enough to leave a trail on the surface when the whisk is lifted. Remove from the heat and continue whisking until cool.
4 Sift the flours and cocoa powder together into a bowl. Fold half the flour mixture into the egg mixture with a metal spoon.
5 Pour half the cooled butter around the edge of the mixture and fold in very gently. Gradually fold in the remaining butter and flour alternately. Fold in very lightly or the butter will sink and the result will be a heavy cake. Pour the mixture into the prepared tin.
6 Bake in the oven at 180°C (350°F) mark 4 for 35–40 minutes or until well risen, firm to the touch and beginning to shrink away from the sides of the tin. Turn out on to a wire rack and leave to cool.
7 To make the filling, melt the chocolate (see page 12) and pour it into a food processor with the chestnut purée, cream and brandy. Blend until smooth, then turn into a bowl and leave for a few minutes to cool and thicken slightly.
8 Carefully slice the cake horizontally into four layers and sandwich them back together with a little of the chestnut cream. Cover the top and sides with the remaining cream and mark in a decorative pattern with a palette knife. Decorate with the chestnuts dipped in grated chocolate. Dust the gâteau lightly with a little icing sugar.

DOBOS TORTE

The old Austro-Hungarian empire is the home of this elaborate 'drum cake'. Versions of the traditional sponge rounds, layered with chocolate cream and glazed with caramel, are still to be found in the best cafés and pastry shops from Vienna to Budapest. Be sure to mark the caramel into portions before it hardens or it will be extremely difficult to cut.

SERVES 8

4 eggs
275 g (10 oz) caster sugar
150 g (5 oz) plain flour

For the filling and coating
125 g (4 oz) plain chocolate
3 egg whites
175 g (6 oz) icing sugar, sifted
225 g (8 oz) butter, softened
*125 g (4 oz) crushed biscuits or
chopped nuts*

1 Draw two 20.5 cm (8 inch) circles on two sheets of non-stick baking parchment. Invert the paper on to two baking sheets (so that the pencil marks are underneath).

2 Using a hand-held electric whisk, whisk the eggs and 175 g (6 oz) of the caster sugar in a bowl standing over a saucepan of hot water. Whisk until the mixture is thick enough to leave a trail on the surface when the whisk is lifted. Remove from the heat.

3 Sift half the flour on to the mixture and fold in lightly with a metal spoon. Add the remaining flour in the same way. Carefully spread some of the mixture out on the prepared baking sheets to fill the circles marked on the baking parchment.

4 Bake in the oven at 190°C (375°F) mark 5 for 7–10 minutes or until golden brown. Loosen from the baking parchment and trim each round to a neat shape with a sharp knife. Transfer them to wire racks and leave to cool for about 15 minutes.

5 Re-line the baking sheets with more marked parchment and spread on more mixture. Bake, trim and cool as before. There should be enough mixture to make six or seven rounds.

6 Select the round with the best surface and lay it on an oiled baking sheet.

7 Put the remaining caster sugar in a small, heavy-based saucepan. Heat gently, without stirring, until the sugar has dissolved, then bring to the boil and boil steadily to a rich brown caramel.

8 Pour the caramel over the round on the baking sheet, spreading it with a knife brushed with oil. Mark into eight sections and trim round the edge.

9 To make the filling and coating, melt the chocolate (see page 12) and leave to cool slightly.

10 Put the egg whites and icing sugar in a heatproof bowl standing over a pan of simmering water. Whisk until very thick, then remove from the heat.

11 Put the butter in a bowl and beat until pale and very soft. Gradually beat in the egg and sugar mixture, then stir in the melted chocolate.

12 Sandwich the remaining biscuit rounds together with some of the filling and put the caramel-covered one on top.

13 Spread the sides of the torte with the remaining filling and press the crushed biscuit crumbs or chopped nuts into it to coat the sides.

WHITE CHOCOLATE GÂTEAU

This rich gâteau, covered in a mass of white chocolate curls, is a scaled-down version of the wedding cake on page 32.

SERVES 18–20

23 cm (9 inch) baked chocolate genoese (see page 52)

For the filling
175 g (6 oz) plain chocolate
30 ml (2 tbsp) orange-flavoured liqueur
2 eggs, separated
300 ml (½ pint) double cream
5 ml (1 level tsp) powdered gelatine

For the decoration
150 ml (¼ pint) double cream
large chocolate curls made from 450 g (1 lb) white chocolate (see page 13)
icing sugar and cocoa powder for dusting

1 To make the filling, melt the chocolate (see page 12), then remove from the heat and stir in the liqueur and egg yolks. Whip the cream until it just stands in soft peaks, then fold into the chocolate mixture.

2 Sprinkle the gelatine over 15 ml (1 tbsp) water in a small heatproof bowl and leave to soak for 2–3 minutes. Place the bowl over a saucepan of simmering water and stir until the gelatine has dissolved. Cool, then stir into the chocolate mixture. Whisk the egg whites until stiff, then fold in.

3 Cut the cake horizontally into two layers. Put one piece of sponge back in the tin and pour the mousse filling on top. Put the second piece of sponge on top. Leave to set.

4 When the mousse is set, whip the cream for the decoration until it holds its shape. Ease the cake out of the tin and cover with the cream. Cover completely with chocolate curls and dust lightly with icing sugar and cocoa powder.

SACHERTORTE

Famous the world over, Sachertorte was the invention of Franz Sacher, a master sugar baker, in Vienna in 1832. It is a very rich, moist chocolate cake. This version is not entirely authentic, but it is the one we found most delicious.

SERVES 8–10

150 g (5 oz) plain chocolate
125 g (4 oz) unsalted butter or
margarine, softened
125 g (4 oz) caster sugar
125 g (4 oz) ground almonds
4 eggs, separated
50 g (2 oz) fresh brown
breadcrumbs
30 ml (2 tbsp) apricot jam, melted

For the icing
200 g (7 oz) plain chocolate
200 ml (7 fl oz) double cream

1 Grease a 23 cm (9 inch) spring-release cake tin, line with greaseproof paper and grease the paper.
2 To make the cake, melt the chocolate (see page 12), then remove from the heat and leave to cool slightly.
3 Cream the butter and sugar together until pale and fluffy. Stir in the almonds, egg yolks, breadcrumbs and melted chocolate, then beat until well combined.
4 Whisk the egg whites until stiff and fold half into the chocolate mixture, then fold in the other half. Pour the mixture into the prepared tin and level the surface.
5 Bake in the oven at 180°C (350°F) mark 4 for 40–45 minutes or until firm to the touch.
6 Cover with a clean, damp tea-towel, leave for 5 minutes to cool slightly, then unclip the sides of the tin and invert the cake on to a wire rack. Remove the base of the tin. Turn the cake the right way up, cover again and leave to cool. When cold, brush the top with melted apricot jam.
7 To make the icing, break the chocolate into small pieces and place it in a heatproof bowl with the cream. Stand the bowl over a saucepan of simmering water and heat until the chocolate melts and blends with the cream. Cool until the icing just coats the back of a spoon.
8 Stand the cake and the wire rack on a baking sheet and pour over the icing. Gently shake the cake to spread the icing evenly and use a palette knife, if necessary, to ensure that the sides are completely covered. Leave in a cool place to set, but do not put in the refrigerator or the icing will lose its shine.

CHOCOLATE-WRAPPED ORANGE LIQUEUR GÂTEAU

For this unusual gâteau, the sponge is soaked in a liqueur syrup, and wrapped in an intriguing chocolate frill that is easier to make than it looks. Chocolate modelling paste (see page 17) works equally well.

SERVES 12

200 g (7 oz) self-raising flour
50 g (2 oz) cornflour
7.5 ml (1½ level tsp) baking powder
175 g (6 oz) caster sugar
3 eggs, separated
finely grated rind and juice of
1 small orange
105 ml (7 tbsp) sunflower oil
45 ml (3 tbsp) milk

For the liqueur syrup
125 g (4 oz) granulated sugar
finely grated rind and juice of
1 orange
45 ml (3 tbsp) orange-flavoured
liqueur

For the decoration
2 large oranges
300 ml (½ pint) double cream
225 g (8 oz) plain chocolate
cocoa powder for dusting

1 Grease a deep 22 cm (8½ inch) spring-release cake tin and line the base with greaseproof paper.

2 Mix the flours, baking powder and sugar together in a bowl. Blend the egg yolks with the orange rind and juice, oil and milk, then mix into the dry ingredients. Beat thoroughly with a wooden spoon to make a smooth batter. Whisk the egg whites until stiff, then fold into the mixture. Pour into the prepared tin.

3 Bake in the oven at 180°C (350°F) mark 4 for about 55 minutes or until well risen and firm to the touch.

4 Meanwhile, to make the syrup, put the sugar, orange rind and juice and 60 ml (4 tbsp) water in a heavy-based saucepan and heat gently until the sugar has dissolved. Bring to the boil and boil rapidly for 2 minutes. Stir in the liqueur.

5 Prick the hot cake all over with a fork, then spoon over the hot syrup. Leave to cool.

6 To make the decoration, peel the oranges, discarding all of the white pith. Roughly chop the flesh. Whip the cream until if forms soft peaks.

7 Remove the cooled cake from the tin and place it on a serving plate. Arrange the chopped orange on top. Spread the cream all over the top and sides.

8 Melt the chocolate (see page 12).

9 Meanwhile, cut a strip of greaseproof paper long enough to go round the sides of the cake and wide enough to come 4 cm (1½ inches) above the cake. When the chocolate has melted, spread it evenly all over the paper with a palette knife. Leave to cool until no longer runny but still sticky when pressed with a finger.

10 Wrap the chocolate around the gâteau, pressing it gently on to the cream so that it sticks. Carefully pinch the chocolate and paper into loose pleats where it extends above the cake. Leave until set, then carefully peel away the paper. Dust the top with a little cocoa powder.

CHOCOLATE TEMPTATION

The richest of chocolate desserts, this gâteau will keep in the refrigerator for 3–4 days, where it will gradually become more fudge-like.

SERVES 8

250 g (9 oz) plain chocolate
15 ml (1 level tbsp) instant coffee powder
30 ml (2 tbsp) brandy
4 eggs
5 ml (1 tsp) vanilla essence
50 g (2 oz) caster sugar
30 ml (2 level tbsp) cornflour
25 g (1 oz) cocoa powder, sifted
1 quantity Chocolate Ganache (see page 152)
two-tone chocolate curls (see page 13) and icing sugar, to decorate

1 Lightly oil a 1.1 litre (2 pint) capacity loaf tin. Line the base and sides of the tin with non-stick baking parchment.

2 Break the chocolate into a heatproof bowl. Add the coffee powder, brandy and 30 ml (2 tbsp) water. Place the bowl over a saucepan of gently simmering water and heat gently until the chocolate has melted. Stir until smooth, then remove from the heat and set aside to cool.

3 Using an electric whisk, whisk together the eggs, vanilla essence, sugar and cornflour until very thick and pale. Fold in the cool, but not cold, chocolate mixture with the cocoa powder.

4 Pour the mixture into the prepared tin and bake in the oven at 180°C (350°F) mark 4 for about 1 hour or until a skewer inserted in the centre comes out clean. (The cake may be cracked slightly.) Remove from the tin, place on a wire rack and leave to cool.

5 Slice the cake horizontally in half and sandwich the layers back together with two thirds of the ganache. Spread the remaining ganache over the top and sides of the cake. Refrigerate for 10 minutes.

6 Serve immediately, decorated with chocolate curls and icing sugar, or wrap and store in the refrigerator for up to 4 days.

STRAWBERRY ALMOND LAYER GÂTEAU

To make this gâteau, a Swiss roll mixture is cooked and, instead of being rolled up, is cut into three and layered with strawberries and cream. Make a Swiss roll (see page 45), then turn it out on to a sheet of greaseproof paper dredged with caster sugar and leave to cool.

SERVES 8

1 baked Chocolate Swiss Roll (see page 45)

For the filling and decoration
700 g (1½ lb) small strawberries
15 ml (1 level tbsp) icing sugar
30 ml (2 tbsp) strawberry liqueur
75 g (3 oz) plain chocolate
30 ml (2 level tbsp) strawberry jam
450 ml (¾ pint) whipping cream
a few drops of almond essence
75 g (3 oz) flaked almonds, toasted

1 Hull and slice 450 g (1 lb) of the strawberries and put them in a bowl with the icing sugar and liqueur. Leave to stand for 20 minutes, stirring the strawberries gently from time to time.

2 Meanwhile, trim the edges of the Swiss roll, then cut widthways into three even pieces. Melt the chocolate (see page 12) and leave to cool slightly.

3 Halve the remaining strawberries (leaving the stalks attached). Dip the base of each piece of strawberry in the chocolate. Leave to set on greaseproof paper.

4 Drain the strawberry slices, reserving the juice. Stir the jam into the juice and mix together. Brush a little of the jam and juice mixture over two pieces of the cake. Top with the strawberry slices.

5 Whip the cream until it stands in soft peaks, then flavour to taste with a little almond essence. Spread a little cream on top of the strawberries.

6 Place the strawberry-covered pieces of cake on top of one another, then cover with the remaining piece of cake. Spread the top and sides with the remaining jam mixture, then cover completely with the cream. Press the toasted nuts on to the sides. Decorate the top of the gâteau with the chocolate-dipped strawberries.

● For maximum volume, leave the eggs at cool room temperature for 2 hours before using.

● Egg whites should be whisked until they form stiff peaks – any further and water will seep out, leaving them dry so that they lose bulk, as they do if left to stand after whisking.

● Traces of egg yolk or grease on the bowl or whisk will prevent the meringue reaching maximum volume and result in a runny meringue that won't pipe successfully. To ensure that the bowl really is grease-free, wipe it out with the cut side of a lemon.

● Insufficient whisking before adding the sugar also results in a runny meringue. If whisked correctly, the whites should stand in stiff peaks that do not fall over at the tip.

● If the baked meringue is smooth on the outside with a hard, close texture, and very soft and chewy inside, or the sugar has bubbled out, the sugar was added too quickly or too much was added at once. If sugar weeps from the cracks, turn the meringue over on to a clean sheet of baking parchment and return it to the oven to dry out. This can even be done the following day.

CINNAMON MERINGUES

Cinnamon meringues freeze successfully, before filling. Simply pack them in a rigid container, with the layers separated by greaseproof paper. Thaw for about 2 hours at room temperature before filling with Chocolate Ganache.

MAKES ABOUT 18

3 egg whites
175 g (6 oz) icing sugar
10 ml (2 level tsp) ground
cinnamon
1 quantity Chocolate Ganache
(see page 152)
icing sugar for dusting

1 Line three baking sheets with non-stick baking parchment.
2 To make the meringue, place the egg whites in a large heatproof bowl. Sift in the icing sugar and cinnamon and stand the bowl over a saucepan of hot water. Using an electric hand-held whisk, beat the egg whites and sugar until the mixture stands in very stiff peaks.
3 Spoon the mixture into a piping bag fitted with a large star nozzle. Secure the paper to the baking sheets with a little meringue. Pipe about 36 fingers of meringue, about 1 cm (½ inch) thick and 7.5 cm (3 inches) long on to the paper.
4 Bake in the oven at 100°C (200°F) mark low for 2½–3 hours or until dry. Swap the baking sheets around during this time so that the meringues cook evenly. Cool on a wire rack.
5 Sandwich the meringue fingers together with Chocolate Ganache and dust with icing sugar to serve.

CHOCOLATE AND GRAND MARNIER MERINGUES

The sultanas will slowly mop up the liqueur, giving them a delicious orange flavour. If you find it easier, use spoons to shape the meringues rather than piping them.

MAKES ABOUT 16

150 g (5 oz) sultanas
45 ml (3 tbsp) Grand Marnier or
Cointreau
4 egg whites
225 g (8 oz) caster sugar
300 ml (½ pint) double cream
200 g (7 oz) plain chocolate
icing sugar for dusting

1 Roughly chop the sultanas and put them in a small bowl with the Grand Marnier. Stir well to mix, then cover and leave to soak for at least 4 hours.

2 Meanwhile, line two baking sheets with non-stick baking parchment. Whisk the egg whites until stiff – the mixture should stand in peaks which just flop over at the top. Whisk in 25 g (1 oz) sugar, keeping the mixture stiff, then gradually fold in the remaining sugar.

3 Spoon the meringue into a piping bag fitted with a 1 cm (½ inch) plain nozzle and pipe it on to the prepared baking sheets, making about 32 meringue shapes in total.

4 Bake in the oven at 100°C (200°F) mark low for about 2 hours or until the meringues are well dried out. Switch the baking sheets around halfway through the cooking time. Carefully peel the meringues off the paper, place on wire racks and leave to cool. When they are quite cold, store in an airtight container until required.

5 About 2 hours before serving, pour 45 ml (3 tbsp) cream into a small saucepan. Whip the remainder until it holds its shape, then fold in the soaked sultanas and any remaining Grand Marnier. Sandwich the meringues together with the cream mixture and pile into a glass serving dish. Grate over a little of the chocolate and dust with icing sugar. Cover and keep in the refrigerator until required.

6 Meanwhile, to make the chocolate sauce, break up the remaining chocolate and add it to the cream in the saucepan. Pour in 150 ml (¼ pint) water and warm gently until the chocolate melts, stirring occasionally. Simmer gently for about 3 minutes, stirring frequently until the sauce thickens slightly. Pour into a jug to serve with the meringues.

MERINGUE AND GANACHE GÂTEAU

This very rich gâteau makes a lovely party-time special.

SERVES 14–16

4 egg whites
225 g (8 oz) caster sugar

For the filling and decoration
350 g (12 oz) plain chocolate
475 ml (16 fl oz) double cream
30–45 ml (2–3 tbsp) brandy or rum
icing sugar for dusting

1 Draw a 20.5 cm (8 inch) circle in the centre of each of four sheets of non-stick baking parchment. Place upside-down on separate baking sheets (so the pencil marks are underneath).
2 Whisk the egg whites until stiff but not dry. Gradually whisk in the sugar, a little at a time, whisking well until very stiff and shiny. Divide the meringue equally between the prepared baking sheets, then spread evenly to fill the marked rounds neatly.
3 Bake in the oven at 140°C (275°F) mark 1 for 1–1¼ hours or until dry, swapping over the baking sheets during cooking to ensure the meringue rounds dry out evenly. Leave to cool.
4 Meanwhile, to make the filling, break the chocolate into small pieces and put it in a large saucepan with the cream. Heat gently, stirring, until the chocolate melts and blends with the cream to form a smooth rich cream. Do not allow to boil.
5 Pour the chocolate cream into a bowl and leave to cool, stirring frequently to prevent a skin forming. When cold, add the brandy and whisk well until light and fluffy.
6 Place one of the meringue rounds on a flat serving plate, then spread with a gener-ous layer of the whipped chocolate cream. Continue until all the meringue rounds are sandwiched together.
7 Spread the remaining chocolate cream all over the meringue to cover completely. Mark the cream into swirls with a palette knife. Sift the icing sugar lightly over the gâteau. Put in the refrigerator until slightly chilled, but do not let the chocolate cream set too hard. Serve the gâteau straight from the refrigerator, still slightly chilled.

CHOCOLATE CHIP MERINGUES

Serve these chocolate-speckled meringues with a bowl of fresh raspberries or straw-berries, or a fresh fruit salad.

SERVES 6

4 egg whites
225 g (8 oz) caster sugar
125 g (4 oz) bittersweet chocolate, grated
300 ml (½ pint) double or whipping cream

1 Line a baking sheet with non-stick baking parchment.
2 Whisk the egg whites until stiff but not dry. Whisk in 20 ml (4 tsp) of the caster sugar, keeping the mixture stiff. Fold in the remaining sugar with the grated chocolate.
3 Spoon out 12 meringues on to the pre-pared baking sheet, allowing them room to spread.
4 Bake in the oven at 130°C (250°F) mark ½ for about 1½ hours or until dry. Peel off the paper and cool on a wire rack.
5 To serve, whip the cream until softly stiff and use to sandwich the meringues together.

CHOCOLATE AND CHESTNUT MERINGUE GÂTEAU

The meringues can be made in advance and stored in an airtight container. Do not sandwich them with the filling more than 2 hours before serving or they will become soggy.

SERVES 10–12

175 g (6 oz) shelled hazelnuts
6 egg whites
350 g (12 oz) caster sugar

For the filling and decoration
225 g (8 oz) plain chocolate
60 ml (4 tbsp) dark rum
350 g (12 oz) sweetened chestnut purée
300 ml (½ pint) double or whipping cream
toasted and chopped hazelnuts, to decorate

1 Grease three 20.5 cm (8 inch) round sandwich tins and line the bases with greaseproof paper.

2 Toast the hazelnuts lightly under the grill, shaking the pan frequently. Transfer the nuts to a clean tea-towel and rub gently while still hot to remove the skins. Grind until very fine.

3 Put the egg whites in a large bowl and whisk until very stiff and standing in peaks. Whisk in half of the sugar and continue whisking until the meringue is glossy. Fold in the remaining sugar with the hazelnuts.

4 Divide the meringue between the prepared sandwich tins. Level the tops and bake in the oven at 180°C (350°F) mark 4 for 35–40 minutes or until crisp.

5 Invert the tins on to a wire rack and turn out the meringues. Peel off the lining papers carefully. (Don't worry if the meringues are cracked.) Leave to cool.

6 To make the filling, melt the chocolate with the rum (see page 12). Remove from the heat and gradually blend in 225 g (8 oz) of the chestnut purée.

7 Put one meringue round, soft side uppermost, on a serving plate. Spread with half of the chocolate and chestnut mixture, then top with the second meringue round, crisp side uppermost. Spread with the remaining mixture, then top with the last round, crisp side uppermost.

8 Whip the cream until it holds its shape. Reserve 30 ml (2 tbsp) of the cream and swirl the remainder all over the gâteau to cover the top and sides completely. Blend the remaining chestnut purée into the reserved cream, then pipe around the top edge of the gâteau. Decorate with hazelnuts. Chill in the refrigerator before serving.

CHOCOLATE PAVLOVA

A luscious, squidgy meringue base, topped with cream and a huge pile of chocolate curls. For sheer decadence, add a layer of whipped Chocolate Ganache (see page 152) before the layer of cream and top the chocolate curls with chocolate-dipped straw-berries and a few redcurrants.

SERVES 8–10

3 egg whites (size 1)
175 g (6 oz) caster sugar
5 ml (1 level tsp) cornflour
5 ml (1 tsp) white wine vinegar
150 ml (¼ pint) double cream
300 ml (½ pint) Greek-style yogurt
350 g (12 oz) plain and white
chocolate curls (see page 13), or
grated chocolate
icing sugar for dusting

1 Draw a 23 cm (9 inch) oval on a piece of non-stick baking parchment and place upside-down on a baking sheet.

2 Whisk the egg whites until very stiff. Add one third of the sugar and continue whisking until stiff again. Add another third of the sugar and whisk again. Add the remaining sugar and continue whisking until the meringue forms soft peaks. Fold in the cornflour and vinegar.

3 Pile or pipe the meringue into the oval marked on the baking sheet. Make a hollow in the centre to hold the filling.

4 Bake in the oven at 180°C (350°F) mark 4 for 5 minutes, then reduce the oven temperature to 130°C (250°F) mark ½ and continue baking for a further 45–50 minutes or until the meringue is set but still soft in the middle.

5 Leave to cool slightly, then carefully peel off the paper. Don't worry if the meringue cracks a little at this stage. Leave to cool completely.

6 Whip the cream until it just holds its shape, then fold in the yogurt. Pile on top of the Pavlova and sprinkle with the chocolate curls. Dust the top of the Pavlova with icing sugar.

CHOCOLATE MERINGUE ROULADE

This gooey meringue mixture is baked like a Swiss roll, then filled with cream, chocolate and fruit. Chocolate Ganache (see page 152), thinned with a little cream or milk, could also be used as a filling, or serve the roulade with a hot chocolate sauce (see page 153).

SERVES 6

4 egg whites
225 g (8 oz) caster sugar
150 ml (¼ pint) double cream
icing sugar for dusting
125 g (4 oz) plain or milk
chocolate, coarsely grated
225 g (8 oz) raspberries,
strawberries or a mixture of fresh
fruit, prepared as necessary
cocoa powder for dusting
whipped cream and plain or milk
chocolate caraque (see page 13),
to decorate

1 First prepare the paper case. Cut out two sheets of non-stick baking parchment, each measuring 30.5×38 cm (12×15 inches). Place together, then fold up 2.5 cm (1 inch) all round and snip into the corners. Fold the corners round and pin or staple together, forming a strong, double-thickness paper case. Place on a baking sheet.

2 Whisk the egg whites until they stand in soft peaks. Whisk in half of the sugar, adding about 25 g (1 oz) at a time and whisking thoroughly between each addition so the mixture remains stiff. Fold in the remaining sugar.

3 Spoon the meringue into the paper case, spreading it gently and evenly into the corners.

4 Bake the meringue in the oven at 100°C (200°F) mark low for 40–45 minutes or until it is just tinged with colour and firm yet spongy when lightly pressed. Cool for about 1 hour. Whip the cream until it just holds its shape.

5 Place a large sheet of non-stick baking parchment on a work surface and dust it with icing sugar. Snip open the corners of the paper case and ease the paper away from the roulade using a blunt knife. Flip the roulade on to the baking parchment and carefully peel away the paper. If the meringue sticks, gently scrape it away with the knife and patch it up as necessary.

6 Spread the cream over the roulade and sprinkle with the grated chocolate and the fruit. Roll up the roulade from one of the narrow ends using the paper to help. It will crack a little as it is rolled. Slide it on to a flat serving platter. Dust with cocoa powder and decorate with piped whipped cream and chocolate caraque. Cover loosely and chill in the refrigerator for up to 4 hours before serving.

BROWN SUGAR PECAN MERINGUE CAKE

Chop the nuts roughly, by hand. If they are chopped too finely in a food processor, we found that they spoilt the texture and volume of the meringue.

SERVES 8–10

4 egg whites
125 g (4 oz) caster sugar
125 g (4 oz) light brown soft sugar
125 g (4 oz) pecan nuts, toasted
and roughly chopped

For the filling and decoration
125 g (4 oz) plain chocolate
450 ml (¾ pint) double cream
icing sugar and cocoa powder for
dusting

1 Draw a 23 cm (9 inch) circle on each of two sheets of non-stick baking parchment. Place the paper upside-down on two baking sheets (so that the pencil marks are underneath).

2 Using a hand-held electric whisk, whisk the egg whites until they stand in soft peaks. Mix together the sugars and add to the egg white, whisking in about 15 ml (1 level tbsp) at a time. Whisk well between each addition until the mixture is stiff. Fold in about three quarters of the nuts.

3 Spread the meringue mixture into the rounds marked on the baking parchment. Sprinkle the remaining chopped nuts over one meringue.

4 Bake in the oven at 150°C (300°F) mark 2 for about 1½ hours or until the meringue is just set and firm to the touch. When quite cold, peel off the non-stick paper.

5 Meanwhile, prepare the filling. Break up the chocolate and place it in a small saucepan with 150 ml (¼ pint) of the cream. Warm gently until the chocolate melts, stirring occasionally. Bring to the boil, stirring, then remove from the heat. Cool, cover and refrigerate until required.

6 About 1 hour before using, remove the chocolate filling from the refrigerator and leave to soften, then carefully spread it over the plain meringue round. Whip the remaining cream and spread it over the chocolate. Finish with the nut-topped meringue round. Refrigerate for 2–3 hours before serving, dusted with icing sugar and cocoa powder.

CRISP CHOCOLATE MERINGUES

These rounds of meringue are coated with a layer of chocolate and sandwiched with fruit and cream. You'll need to eat them with a spoon and fork.

SERVES 6

3 egg whites
175 g (6 oz) caster sugar
175 g (6 oz) plain or milk chocolate
300 ml (½ pint) double cream
350 g (12 oz) fresh fruit of your
choice, prepared as necessary
cocoa powder, to dredge
piped chocolate shapes
(see page 16), to decorate
Coffee Custard (see page 153),
to serve (optional)

1 Mark twelve 8.5 cm (3½ inch) rounds on two sheets of non-stick baking parchment. Place upside-down on two baking sheets (so the pencil marks are underneath).

2 Whisk the egg whites until stiff, then whisk in half of the sugar. Carefully fold in the remaining sugar with a metal spoon. Spoon the mixture into a piping bag fitted with a large star nozzle and pipe on to the paper, using the circles as a guide.

3 Bake in the oven at 130°C (250°F) mark ½ for about 1½ hours if you like soft meringues, or 2½–3 hours for crisp, dry meringues. Leave to cool slightly, then carefully peel off the paper, place on a wire rack and leave to cool completely.

4 Melt the chocolate (see page 12) and leave to cool slightly, then spread over the undersides of the meringues. Return to the wire rack and leave to set.

5 Whip the cream until it just holds its shape. Pipe or spread a little of it on to six of the meringue rounds (on top of the chocolate). Top with one of the remaining meringues, chocolate side down.

6 Spread the meringues with more cream and top with the prepared fruit. Dredge with cocoa powder and decorate with chocolate shapes. Serve each meringue on a pool of coffee custard, if liked.

CHAPTER THREE

HOT PUDDINGS

CHOCOLATE FILO PIE

An unusual but delicious way to use up stale cake crumbs.

SERVES 9–12

4 large sheets of filo pastry, thawed
if frozen
50 g (2 oz) butter, melted

For the filling
75 g (3 oz) butter, softened
75 g (3 oz) icing sugar
4 eggs, separated
75 g (3 oz) ground almonds
125 g (4 oz) plain or chocolate cake
crumbs
125 g (4 oz) dried mixed fruit
125 g (4 oz) plain chocolate, grated
15 ml (1 level tbsp) cocoa powder,
sifted
150 ml (¼ pint) double cream

For the decoration
50 g (2 oz) flaked almonds
15 ml (1 level tbsp) icing sugar,
sifted

1 To make the filling, cream the butter and icing sugar together until pale and fluffy. Gradually beat in the egg yolks, then the almonds, cake crumbs, mixed fruit, chocolate, cocoa powder and cream. Whisk the egg whites until stiff, then fold into the chocolate mixture.

2 Fold one sheet of filo pastry in half and trim to fit a 22 × 28.5 cm (8½ × 11½ inch) baking dish. Repeat with the remaining sheets of pastry, reserving the trimmings.

3 Lay one of the folded sheets of pastry in the dish and spread with one third of the chocolate filling. Cover with a second folded sheet of pastry. Repeat the layers twice more, ending with a pastry layer. Brush the top with the melted butter. Cut the pastry trimmings into neat strips and sprinkle on top. Brush with more melted butter and sprinkle with the almonds and icing sugar.

4 Bake in the oven at 190°C (375°F) mark 5 for 40 minutes or until golden brown. Serve hot or cold, cut into squares, with vanilla ice cream.

BAKED CHOCOLATE MARBLE SPONGE

A delicious family pudding to serve on cold winter days.

SERVES 8

75 g (3 oz) plain chocolate
175 g (6 oz) butter or margarine,
softened
175 g (6 oz) light brown soft sugar
3 eggs, beaten
200 g (7 oz) self-raising flour
45 ml (3 tbsp) milk
50 g (2 oz) macaroons

1 Grease a 1.3 litre (2¼ pint) loaf dish.

2 Melt the chocolate (see page 12) and leave until cool (but not set).

3 Meanwhile, cream the butter and sugar together until pale and fluffy. Gradually beat in the eggs, beating well after each addition, then fold in the flour and milk.

4 Divide the mixture in two and flavour half with the melted chocolate, folding it evenly through the mixture.

5 Place alternate spoonfuls of the mixtures in two layers in the prepared dish and zig-zag a knife through the mixture to create a marbled pattern. Roughly crush the macaroons and scatter them over the top. Cover with foil.

6 Bake in the oven at 180°C (350°F) mark 4 for about 1¼ hours or until firm to the touch. Turn out and serve thickly sliced with Chocolate Custard Sauce or Chocolate Fudge Sauce (see page 153).

CHOCOLATE CINNAMON CRÊPES

This makes ten generously filled crêpes, enough for five, allowing two each.

SERVES 5

125 g (4 oz) plain flour
a pinch of salt
10 ml (2 level tsp) ground cinnamon
1 egg
300 ml (½ pint) milk
oil for frying
grated white and plain chocolate, to decorate

For the filling
125 g (4 oz) plain flour
50 g (2 oz) caster sugar
5 ml (1 level tsp) ground cinnamon
300 ml (½ pint) milk
50 g (2 oz) plain chocolate, chopped
grated rind of 1 lemon
4 eggs, separated

1 Sift the flour, salt and cinnamon into a bowl and make a well in the centre. Break in the egg and beat well with a wooden spoon. Gradually beat in the milk, drawing in the flour from the sides to make a smooth batter.

2 Heat a little oil in an 18 cm (7 inch) pancake pan, running it around the base and sides of the pan, until hot. Pour off any surplus.

3 Pour in just enough batter to coat the base of the pan thinly. Cook for 1–2 minutes or until golden brown underneath. Turn or toss and cook the second side until golden.

4 Transfer the pancake to a plate and keep hot. Repeat with the remaining batter to make ten pancakes. Pile the cooked pancakes on top of each other with greaseproof paper in between each one and keep warm in the oven while cooking the remainder.

5 To make the filling, mix the flour, sugar and cinnamon together in a bowl. Blend to a smooth paste with a little of the milk. Heat the remaining milk to boiling point and whisk in the flour mixture. Bring to the boil, whisking all the time until very thick. Remove from the heat.

6 Stir the chocolate and lemon rind into the mixture until completely blended and smooth. Gradually beat in the egg yolks. Whisk the egg whites until stiff, then fold into the mixture.

7 Spoon about 60 ml (4 tbsp) filling mixture on the centre of each crêpe. Fold in the sides to enclose completely. Arrange the crêpes, seam side downwards in a single layer, in a greased ovenproof dish.

8 Bake in the oven at 220ºC (425ºF) mark 7 for 15–20 minutes or until the filling is just set. Serve hot or cold, decorated with grated white and plain chocolate.

FRESH FRUIT WITH HOT CHOCOLATE AND CREAMY FUDGE DIPS

Keep the dips hot over simmering water until you're ready to serve.

SERVES 6–8

50 g (2 oz) fudge-filled chocolate bars (such as 5 small Cadbury's bars)
90 ml (6 tbsp) single cream
125 g (4 oz) plain chocolate
a knob of butter
prepared fresh fruits, such as seedless grapes, pineapple, bananas, apples, pears
single cream or chocolate, to decorate

1 For the Creamy Fudge Dip, break the fudge-filled chocolate bars into small pieces and place in a small heatproof bowl. Add the cream. Place over a saucepan of gently simmering water until completely melted, stirring occasionally until smooth.

2 For the Hot Chocolate Dip, melt the plain chocolate with 45 ml (3 tbsp) water (see page 12). Add the butter and stir until smooth.

3 Arrange the prepared fruits around the edge of a large platter. Place the Hot Chocolate and Creamy Fudge Dips in the centre. Decorate the surfaces of the Dips with swirls of cream or grated chocolate. Serve immediately.

STICKY UPSIDE-DOWN PUDDING

SERVES 8

275 g (10 oz) plain chocolate
75 g (3 oz) pecan nuts
125 g (4 oz) butter or margarine
2 eggs
75 g (3 oz) caster sugar
2.5 ml (½ tsp) vanilla essence
15 ml (1 tbsp) strong black coffee
75 g (3 oz) self-raising flour
700 g (1½ lb) ripe pears or two 400 g (14 oz) cans pear quarters, drained

1 Grease a 1.1 litre (2 pint), 23 cm (9 inch) round ovenproof dish and line the base with non-stick baking parchment. Roughly chop 75 g (3 oz) of the chocolate and the nuts. Melt the remaining chocolate with the butter (see page 12), then remove from the heat and leave to cool slightly.

2 Beat together the eggs, sugar, vanilla essence, coffee and melted chocolate. Fold in the flour, chopped chocolate and nuts, and mix well.

3 Peel, quarter and core the pears and arrange them in the prepared dish. Pour over the chocolate mixture.

4 Bake in the oven at 190°C (375°F) mark 5 for 1 hour, covering with foil after 30 minutes. Cool slightly, then turn out on to a plate and serve with ice cream.

Opposite: Sticky Upside-Down Pudding

INDIVIDUAL CHOCOLATE MINT SOUFFLÉS

For added luxury, pour in a little single cream to serve.

SERVES 4–6

150 ml (¼ pint) milk
12 After Eight mints
25 g (1 oz) butter or margarine
20 g (¾ oz) plain flour
25 g (1 oz) caster sugar
3 eggs, separated

1 Lightly grease six 150 ml (¼ pint) ramekin dishes.
2 Heat the milk and mints in a saucepan until evenly blended.
3 Melt the butter in a large heavy-based saucepan. Add the flour and cook for 1 minute, then remove from the heat and gradually blend in the milk and mint mixture. Bring to the boil, stirring all the time, and cook for 1 minute.
4 Cool slightly, then beat in the sugar and egg yolks.
5 Whisk the egg whites until stiff but not dry. Beat one spoonful into the sauce to lighten it, then carefully fold in the remaining egg white. Spoon into the prepared dishes. Stand the dishes on a baking sheet.
6 Bake in the oven at 190°C (375°F) mark 5 for 15–20 minutes or until lightly set. Serve straight away.

CHOCOLATE CINNAMON SOUFFLÉ

If you like your soufflé soft in the middle, cook it for the minimum time given here; if you prefer it set throughout, cook for at least 40 minutes.

SERVES 4

75 g (3 oz) plain chocolate
300 ml (½ pint) plus 15 ml (1 tbsp) milk
50 g (2 oz) butter or margarine
40 g (1½ oz) plain flour
2.5 ml (½ level tsp) ground cinnamon
5 eggs, separated
25 g (1 oz) caster sugar
icing sugar for dusting

1 Tie a double strip of greaseproof paper around a 1.4 litre (2½ pint) soufflé dish to make a 7.5 cm (3 inch) collar. Brush the inside with melted butter.
2 Melt the chocolate with the 15 ml (1 tbsp) milk (see page 12). Remove from the heat.
3 Melt the butter in a large heavy-based saucepan. Add the flour and cook for 1 minute, then remove from the heat and gradually blend in the remaining milk and the cinnamon. Bring to the boil, stirring all the time, and cook for about 1 minute.
4 Cool slightly, then beat in the egg yolks, sugar and melted chocolate.
5 Whisk the egg whites until stiff but not dry. Beat one spoonful into the sauce mixture to lighten it, then carefully fold in the remaining egg whites.
6 Gently pour the soufflé mixture into the prepared dish and level the top. Stand the dish on a baking sheet.
7 Bake in the oven at 190°C (375°F) mark 5 for 35–40 minutes or until well risen, just set and well browned. Remove the paper and dust lightly with icing sugar. Serve straight away.

POIRES BELLE HÉLÈNE

SERVES 6

125 g (4 oz) sugar
thinly pared rind and juice of
2 oranges
6 cooking pears (preferably
Conference)
225 g (8 oz) plain chocolate
60 ml (4 tbsp) orange-flavoured
liqueur
orange slices, to decorate

1 Put the sugar, 900 ml (1½ pints) water and half the orange rind in a large, heavy-based saucepan and heat gently, without stirring, until the sugar has dissolved.

2 Meanwhile, peel the pears quickly, leaving the stalks on. Cut out the cores from the bottom and level the bases.

3 Stand the pears in the syrup, cover the pan and simmer gently for 20 minutes or until tender. Leave to cool, covered, basting occasionally with the syrup.

4 Cut the remaining orange rind into thin matchstick (julienne) strips. Blanch in boiling water for 2 minutes, then drain and immediately refresh under cold running water. Leave to drain on absorbent kitchen paper.

5 Melt the chocolate with the liqueur (see page 12) and leave to cool slightly.

6 Remove the pears from the syrup and stand them on a large serving dish or six individual dishes. Chill for 2 hours.

7 Discard the orange rind from the syrup. Stir the melted chocolate into 150 ml (¼ pint) of the syrup with the orange juice, then slowly bring to the boil, stirring constantly. Simmer, stirring, until the sauce is thick and syrupy.

8 To serve, pour the hot chocolate sauce over the cold pears and sprinkle with the orange julienne. Decorate with orange slices and serve immediately.

STEAMED CHOCOLATE PUDDING

Serve with vanilla ice cream or one of the sauces on page 153. Make the sauce while the pudding is steaming and reheat just before serving.

SERVES 4

50 g (2 oz) plain chocolate
15 ml (1 level tbsp) cocoa powder,
sifted
90 ml (6 tbsp) milk
50 g (2 oz) fresh white breadcrumbs
125 g (4 oz) butter or margarine,
softened
125 g (4 oz) caster sugar
2 eggs
125 g (4 oz) self-raising flour

1 Half-fill a large saucepan or steamer with water and bring to the boil. Grease a 1.1 litre (2 pint) pudding basin. Melt the chocolate (see page 12), then blend in the cocoa powder with 15 ml (1 tbsp) of the milk.

2 Put the breadcrumbs in a small bowl and pour over the remaining milk. Leave to soak.

3 Meanwhile, cream the butter and sugar together until pale and fluffy. Beat in the eggs, flour, melted chocolate and soaked breadcrumbs. Spoon into the prepared basin and make a slight hollow in the centre. Cover with greased greaseproof paper and foil, and secure with string. Put the basin in the saucepan or steamer and cover with a tightly fitting lid. Steam for about 2 hours or until well risen and firm to the touch, adding more boiling water to the pan as necessary.

4 Carefully loosen the pudding from the basin, turn out and serve with your chosen sauce or ice cream.

CHOCOLATE PECAN PIE

Pecan nuts are native to the Mississippi valley; their flavour is somewhat like walnuts, but pecans are oilier. Look for pecans in health food shops, delicatessens and some supermarkets. Walnuts can be used instead.

SERVES 10

For the pastry
275 g (10 oz) plain flour
45 ml (3 level tbsp) cocoa powder
a pinch of salt
150 g (5 oz) unsalted butter, diced
30 ml (2 level tbsp) caster sugar

For the filling
200 g (7 oz) shelled pecan nuts
3 eggs, beaten
225 g (8 oz) light brown soft sugar
250 ml (8 fl oz) evaporated milk
5 ml (1 tsp) vanilla essence
50 g (2 oz) unsalted butter, melted

1 To make the pastry, sift the flour, cocoa powder and salt into a large bowl. Add the diced butter and rub it in with your fingertips until the mixture resembles coarse breadcrumbs. Stir in the sugar. Gradually add 2–3 tablespoons cold water until the dough begins to hold together (it will still be quite crumbly).

2 Turn the dough out on to a lightly floured surface, shape it into a ball, then roll it out and use it to line a lightly greased 28 cm (11 inch) fluted flan tin with a removable base. Prick the pastry all over with a fork, then chill in the refrigerator for 1 hour.

3 Line the pastry with foil and fill with baking beans. Bake blind in the oven at 190°C (375°F) mark 5 for 10 minutes. Remove the foil and beans, return the pastry case to the oven and bake for a further 5 minutes. Remove from the oven and leave to cool. Reduce the oven temperature to 170°C (325°F) mark 3.

4 To make the filling, chop the pecans, reserving 50 g (2 oz) well-formed halves for the decoration. Put the chopped nuts in a bowl and add the remaining filling ingredients. Mix well and pour into the pastry case. Arrange the remaining pecans over the filling and bake in the oven for about 1 hour or until set in the centre. Serve warm or cold with ice cream or whipped cream.

MARBLED HAZELNUT AND LEMON SPONGE

SERVES 6

*40 g (1½ oz) hazelnuts, skinned
and toasted
125 g (4 oz) soft tub margarine
125 g (4 oz) caster sugar
2 eggs, beaten
175 g (6 oz) self-raising flour
30 ml (2 tbsp) milk
finely grated rind of 1 lemon
30 ml (2 level tbsp) cocoa powder*

1 Half-fill a large saucepan or steamer with water and bring to the boil. Meanwhile, grease a 900 ml (1½ pint) fluted brioche or cake mould with a funnel, or a gugelhupf mould. Cover the top of the hole in the centre with a piece of foil to prevent water seeping in during steaming.
2 Put the nuts in a food processor and process until very finely ground. Tip out into a mixing bowl. Wipe out the food processor with a piece of kitchen paper to remove any remaining nuts. Put the margarine, sugar, eggs, flour and milk in the food processor and process for 2–3 minutes until smooth.
3 Remove half of the mixture and fold it into the ground hazelnuts with the lemon rind. Add the cocoa to the mixture remaining in the food processor and process for 1 minute more or until evenly mixed.
4 Fill the prepared mould with these mixtures, adding them in alternate spoonfuls to create a marbled effect. Level the surface, cover with greased greaseproof paper and foil, and secure with string. Put the mould in the saucepan or steamer and cover with a tightly fitting lid. Steam for about 1½ hours or until well risen and firm to the touch, adding more boiling water to the pan as necessary. Carefully loosen the edges of the pudding from the mould, turn out and serve with custard or chocolate sauce.

COFFEE AND CHOCOLATE FUDGE PUDDING

During cooking, this pudding separates to give its own built-in sauce. It's also good served with chilled soured cream.

SERVES 8

*225 g (8 oz) butter or margarine,
softened
350 g (12 oz) soft brown sugar
2 eggs, beaten
90 ml (6 tbsp) coffee essence
175 g (6 oz) self-raising flour, sifted
50 g (2 oz) cocoa powder
50 g (2 oz) walnuts, chopped
568 ml (1 pint) milk*

1 Cream together the butter and 225 g (8 oz) of the sugar. Gradually beat in the eggs with the coffee essence. Fold in the flour and cocoa powder with the walnuts, adding a little of the milk to give a soft dropping consistency.
2 Spoon into a 2.3 litre (4 pint) buttered ovenproof dish.
3 Blend together the remaining brown sugar and the milk, and pour evenly over the pudding mixture. Bake in the oven at 170°C (325°F) mark 3 for about 1 hour 40 minutes or until spongy to the touch.

STEAMED CHOCOLATE SOUFFLÉ WITH CHOCOLATE SAUCE

SERVES 6

25 g (1 oz) unsalted butter
25 g (1 oz) plain flour
150 ml (¼ pint) milk
75 g (3 oz) plain chocolate,
finely chopped
25 g (1 oz) caster sugar
75 ml (3 fl oz) double cream
3 eggs, separated
icing sugar for dusting

For the chocolate sauce
125 g (4 oz) plain chocolate,
finely chopped
30 ml (2 tbsp) brandy
150 ml (¼ pint) double cream
150 ml (¼ pint) milk
15 g (½ oz) unsalted butter
10 ml (2 level tsp) cornflour

1 Grease a 15 cm (6 inch), 7.5 cm (3 inch) deep soufflé dish with butter, then coat evenly with a little caster sugar.

2 Melt the butter in a saucepan, then stir in the flour. Remove from the heat and gradually stir in the milk, then add the chocolate. Heat gently, stirring all the time, until the chocolate melts, then cook until thickened. Remove the sauce from the heat, beat in half the sugar, then beat in the cream and the egg yolks.

3 Whisk the egg whites until stiff, but not dry, then gradually whisk in the remaining sugar, whisking until shiny. Add about one third of the egg whites to the chocolate mixture and fold in carefully to loosen the mixture, then very gently fold in the remaining egg whites.

4 Pour the soufflé mixture into the prepared dish. Place a trivet or an up-turned saucer in a heavy-based saucepan, stand the soufflé dish on the trivet, then add enough boiling water to come about one third of the way up the side of the dish. Cover the pan with a tightly fitting lid, then steam the soufflé gently for 45 minutes or until it is well risen and set, adding more boiling water to the saucepan if necessary.

5 Meanwhile, to make the chocolate sauce, put the chocolate, brandy, cream and most of the milk into a small saucepan. Heat gently, stirring until the chocolate melts, then stir in the butter.

6 Blend the cornflour with the remaining milk to form a smooth paste, then stir it into the sauce. Cook over a moderate heat until the sauce thickens slightly. Keep the sauce warm until ready to serve.

7 When the soufflé is cooked, turn the heat off under the pan and allow the soufflé to settle for 5 minutes (it will sink slightly). Turn the soufflé out on to a warmed serving dish and dust with icing sugar. Serve immediately, with the chocolate sauce poured around it, or serve the sauce separately in a warmed jug.

CHOCOLATE MERINGUE PIE

When meringue is grilled, as it is in this recipe, it becomes delightfully soft and mallowy. If you wish to make the pie in advance, leave the chocolate filling to cool with a piece of greaseproof paper lying on its surface to prevent a skin forming.

SERVES 8–10

one 23 cm (9 inch) Shortcrust
Pastry Tart Case (see page 84)

For the filling
25 g (1 oz) caster sugar
40 g (1½ oz) plain flour
25 g (1 oz) cocoa powder
a pinch of salt
450 ml (¾ pint) milk
125 g (4 oz) plain chocolate, finely chopped
3 egg yolks
5 ml (1 tsp) vanilla essence

For the meringue
3 egg whites
175 g (6 oz) caster sugar

1 To make the filling, put the sugar, flour, cocoa powder, salt, milk and chocolate in a heavy-based saucepan and heat very gently, stirring all the time. When the chocolate has melted, increase the heat and cook for about 5 minutes or until boiling and thickened, whisking continuously.
2 Beat the egg yolks with the vanilla essence, then gradually whisk in about half of the chocolate sauce. Return the mixture to the saucepan and heat very gently for 1–2 minutes or until thickened further. (Do not allow this mixture to boil or it will curdle.) Pour the chocolate mixture into the cold pastry case.
3 To make the meringue, whisk the egg whites until stiff, preferably with an electric whisk, then add half of the sugar. Continue whisking until the mixture is smooth and glossy, then gradually fold in the remaining sugar.
4 Preheat the grill to high. Pile the meringue on top of the chocolate mixture, making sure that it completely covers the filling and the pastry edge. Place the pie on the base of the grill, rather than in the grill pan, and cook the meringue under the hot grill for 2–3 minutes or until golden brown and set. Serve immediately.

BLACK BREAD PUDDING

This unlikely combination of flavours makes an interesting bread pudding. It also works well with other tart fruits, such as redcurrants and cranberries.

SERVES 6

3 eggs, separated
125 g (4 oz) caster sugar
2.5 ml (½ level tsp) ground cinnamon
a pinch of salt
350 g (12 oz) dark rye breadcrumbs
125 g (4 oz) plain chocolate, grated
350 g (12 oz) blackcurrants, stalks removed
25 g (1 oz) light brown soft sugar
icing sugar for dusting

1 Grease a 20.5 cm (8 inch) soufflé dish.
2 Whisk the egg yolks, caster sugar and cinnamon together until pale and fluffy.
3 Whisk the egg whites and salt until stiff, then fold into the egg yolk mixture with the breadcrumbs and chocolate. Arrange the blackcurrants in the base of the prepared dish and sprinkle with the brown sugar. Pour the bread mixture over the fruit.
4 Bake in the oven at 180°C (350°F) mark 4 for 40 minutes or until firm to the touch. Dust with icing sugar and serve hot or cold with soured cream.

CHAPTER FOUR
COLD DESSERTS

PÂTE SUCRÉE TART CASE

MAKES ONE 23 CM (9 INCH) TART CASE

225 g (8 oz) plain flour
2.5 ml (½ level tsp) salt
75 g (3 oz) butter, chilled and diced
75 g (3 oz) caster sugar
4 egg yolks
2.5 ml (½ tsp) vanilla essence

1 Sift the flour and salt on to a work surface. Make a well in the centre and add the remaining ingredients.
2 Using the fingertips of one hand, pinch and work the sugar, butter and egg yolks together until well blended.
3 Gradually work in all the flour to bind the mixture together. Knead lightly until smooth.
4 Wrap the pastry in foil or cling film and leave to 'rest' in the refrigerator or a cool place for about 30 minutes.
5 Roll out the pastry on a lightly floured surface and use to line a 23 cm (9 inch) fluted flan tin. Prick the base of the dough. Cut out a piece of greaseproof paper or foil larger than the pastry case. Lay the paper or foil in the pastry case and fill with baking beans to weigh it down.
6 Bake in the oven at 220°C (425°F) mark 7 for 10 minutes, then reduce the oven temperature to 190°C (375°F) mark 5 and bake for a further 5–10 minutes or until lightly browned.
7 If the recipe calls for a completely baked pastry case, remove the paper and beans and bake for a further 5 minutes. Cool slightly in the tin, then remove and cool on a wire rack.

SHORTCRUST PASTRY TART CASE

MAKES ONE 23 CM (9 INCH) TART CASE

125 g (4 oz) butter or margarine
225 g (8 oz) plain flour
a pinch of salt

1 Rub the butter into the flour and salt until the mixture resembles fine breadcrumbs. Add 45–60 ml (3–4 tbsp) chilled water and stir in with a round-bladed knife until the mixture comes together.
2 Knead lightly to make a firm, smooth dough, taking care not to over-handle the dough or the pastry will be tough.
3 Roll out the dough on a lightly floured surface and use to line a 23 cm (9 inch) fluted flan tin. Cover with foil and 'rest' in the refrigerator for 30 minutes before lining with paper or foil weighed down with baking beans and baking blind as for the Pâte Sucrée Tart Case (see left).

CHILLED ITALIAN CHEESECAKE

This cake is best made a day or two before serving and chilled overnight. If your food processor is small, you will have to blend the cheese filling and the crumble topping in two batches.

SERVES 10

75 g (3 oz) shelled hazelnuts
125 g (4 oz) plain chocolate,
roughly chopped
grated rind and juice of 1 lemon
700 g (1½ lb) ricotta cheese
30 ml (2 tbsp) dark rum
175 g (6 oz) caster sugar
2 eggs, plus 1 egg white
200 g (7 oz) cold butter
350 g (12 oz) plain flour
12.5 ml (2½ level tsp) baking powder
125 g (4 oz) soft brown sugar
65 g (2½ oz) ground almonds
5 ml (1 tsp) vanilla essence
icing sugar for dusting

1 Grease a 23 cm (9 inch) deep loose-based cake tin or spring-release cake tin and line the base with non-stick baking parchment.

2 Toast the hazelnuts under a hot grill until browned, place in a tea-towel and rub off the skins. Cool, then place in a food processor with the chocolate, lemon rind and lemon juice, the cheese, rum and sugar. Process until just combined, then turn out into a large bowl. Lightly whisk the extra egg white until it just holds its shape and fold it into the mixture.

3 Cut the butter into 15 g (½ oz) portions and place in the food processor with the flour, baking powder, brown sugar, almonds, vanilla essence and eggs. Process until the mixture resembles coarse breadcrumbs.

4 Spoon one third of the crumb mixture into the base of the prepared cake tin and lightly press into place. Top with the ricotta mixture, levelling the surface, then spoon over the remaining crumb mixture and spread evenly. Make sure the surface is covered but leave the top of the cheesecake quite rough.

5 Stand the tin on a baking sheet and bake in the oven at 180°C (350°F) mark 4 for about 1 hour or until slightly risen, golden brown and firm to the touch. Allow to cool in the tin, then cover and refrigerate overnight.

6 Before serving, take the cake out of the refrigerator and remove it from the tin. Leave at room temperature for about 1 hour before serving dusted with icing sugar.

CHOCOLATE ROULADE

Don't worry if the roulade cracks as you roll it – the cracks are part of its charm.

SERVES 8–10

For the roulade
125 g (4 oz) plain chocolate
4 eggs, separated
125 g (4 oz) caster sugar
30 ml (2 level tbsp) cocoa powder,
sifted

For the filling
150 ml (¼ pint) double cream
15 ml (1 level tbsp) icing sugar
150 ml (¼ pint) Greek-style yogurt
a few drops of rose water (optional)
225 g (8 oz) raspberries

For the sauce and decoration
450 g (1 lb) raspberries
15 ml (1 tbsp) kirsch
icing sugar
white chocolate curls (see page 13)
a few raspberry or mint leaves

1 Grease a 23 × 33 cm (9 × 13 inch) Swiss roll tin, line with greaseproof paper and grease the paper.
2 To make the roulade, melt the chocolate (see page 12) and leave to cool slightly.
3 Whisk the egg yolks and sugar together in a bowl until very thick and pale. Beat in the chocolate. Whisk the egg whites until stiff, then fold carefully into the chocolate mixture with the cocoa powder. Pour the mixture into the prepared tin and spread evenly.
4 Bake in the oven at 180°C (350°F) mark 4 for about 20 minutes or until well risen and firm to the touch.
5 While the roulade is cooking, lay a piece of greaseproof paper on a flat work surface and sprinkle generously with caster sugar. When the roulade is cooked, turn it out on to the paper. Carefully peel off the lining paper. Cover the roulade with a clean, damp tea-towel and leave to cool.
6 To make the filling, whip the cream with the icing sugar until it forms soft peaks. Fold in the yogurt with a few drops of rose water, if using. Spread the cream over the roulade. Sprinkle with the raspberries. Starting from one of the narrow ends, carefully roll up the roulade, using the paper to help. Transfer the roulade to a serving plate and dust generously with icing sugar.
7 To make the sauce, push the raspberries through a sieve, or purée in a blender or food processor, then sieve to make a smooth, seedless purée. Add the liqueur and sweeten to taste with icing sugar.
8 Serve the roulade decorated with icing sugar, white chocolate curls and raspberry or mint leaves, and accompanied by the raspberry sauce.

PROFITEROLES

Always collect the ingredients together before starting to make choux pastry as it is important to add all the flour quickly as soon as the mixture has come to the boil. Raw choux paste is too soft and sticky to be rolled out and is, therefore, piped or spooned on to a dampened baking sheet for baking. During baking, the moisture in the dough turns to steam and puffs up the mixture, leaving the centre hollow. Thorough cooking is important; if insufficiently cooked, the choux may collapse when taken from the oven and there will be uncooked pastry in the centre to scoop out.

SERVES 4

For the choux pastry
65 g (2½ oz) plain or strong flour
50 g (2 oz) butter or margarine
2 eggs, lightly beaten

For the chocolate sauce
125 g (4 oz) plain chocolate
15 g (½ oz) butter or margarine
30 ml (2 tbsp) golden syrup
2–3 drops of vanilla essence

For the filling and decoration
150 ml (¼ pint) double cream
icing sugar for dusting

1 To make the choux pastry, sift the flour on to a plate or piece of paper. Put the butter and 150 ml (¼ pint) water in a saucepan. Heat gently until the butter has melted, then bring to the boil. Remove the pan from the heat and tip the flour all at once into the hot liquid. Beat thoroughly with a wooden spoon.

2 Continue beating the mixture over the heat until it is smooth and forms a ball in the centre of the pan. (Take care not to overbeat or the mixture will become fatty.) Remove from the heat and leave the mixture to cool for 1–2 minutes.

3 Beat in the eggs, a little at a time, adding only just enough to give a piping consistency. It is important to beat the mixture vigorously at this stage to trap in as much air as possible. A hand-held electric mixer is ideal for this purpose. Continue beating until the mixture develops an obvious sheen.

4 Spoon the choux pastry into a piping bag fitted with a 1 cm (½ inch) plain nozzle. Pipe about 20 small bun shapes on two dampened baking sheets.

5 Bake in the oven at 220°C (425°F) mark 7 for 20–25 minutes or until well risen and golden brown. Reduce the oven temperature at 180°C (350°F) mark 4. Remove the buns from the oven and make a hole in the side of each with a skewer or knife to release the steam. Return to the oven for 5 minutes to dry out completely. Leave to cool on a wire rack.

6 To make the chocolate sauce, melt together the chocolate, butter, 30 ml (2 tbsp) water, the golden syrup and vanilla essence in a small saucepan over a very low heat. Stir well until smooth and well blended.

7 Whip the cream until it just holds its shape. Spoon into a piping bag fitted with a medium plain nozzle and use to fill the choux buns through the holes in the sides.

8 Dust the profiteroles with icing sugar and serve with the chocolate sauce spooned over or served separately.

Variation

Chocolate Eclairs Make the choux paste as above, then pipe 6.5 cm (2½ inch) long strips on dampened baking sheets. Bake as above and cool on a wire rack. Fill with cream and dip the tops in melted chocolate or glacé icing made with 125 g (4 oz) icing sugar and 10 ml (2 level tsp) cocoa powder blended with a little hot water.

CHOCOLATE COFFEE REFRIGERATOR SLICE

This quick and easy dessert requires no cooking.

SERVES 6

45 ml (3 tbsp) brandy
250 ml (8 fl oz) freshly made strong
black coffee
125 g (4 oz) plain chocolate
50 g (2 oz) icing sugar
125 g (4 oz) unsalted butter,
softened
2 egg yolks
300 ml (½ pint) whipping cream
50 g (2 oz) chopped almonds,
toasted
about 30 sponge fingers
coffee beans, to decorate

1 Grease a 22×11.5 cm (8½×4½ inch) top measurement loaf tin and line the base with greaseproof paper. Grease the paper. Stir the brandy into the coffee.

2 Melt the chocolate with 15 ml (1 tbsp) water (see page 12). Remove from the heat and leave to cool for about 5 minutes.

3 Sift the icing sugar into a bowl. Add the butter and beat together until pale and fluffy. Add the egg yolks, beating well.

4 Lightly whip the cream and chill half of it. Stir the remaining cream, the cooled chocolate and the nuts into the butter and egg yolk mixture.

5 Line the bottom of the prepared tin with sponge fingers, cutting to fit if necessary. Spoon over one third of the coffee and brandy mixture.

6 Layer the chocolate mixture and remaining sponge fingers in the tin, soaking each layer of sponge fingers with coffee and ending with soaked sponge fingers. Weigh down lightly and chill for 3–4 hours or until set.

7 Turn out, remove the paper and decorate with whipped cream and coffee beans.

CHOCOLATE CUSTARD PIE

SERVES 8

one 23 cm (9 inch) Shortcrust
Pastry Tart Case (see page 84)

For the filling and decoration
125 g (4 oz) caster sugar
50 g (2 oz) plain flour
a pinch of salt
450 ml (¾ pint) milk
50 g (2 oz) plain chocolate
3 egg yolks
40 g (1½ oz) butter or margarine
5 ml (1 tsp) vanilla essence
250 ml (8 fl oz) double or whipping
cream
chocolate curls (see page 13) or
grated chocolate, to decorate

1 To make the filling, mix the sugar, flour and salt in a large saucepan and stir in the milk. Break the chocolate into small pieces and add it to the pan. Heat gently until the chocolate has melted, stirring continuously. Whisk until the chocolate and milk are blended, then increase the heat and cook for about 10 minutes, stirring constantly. Remove the pan from the heat.

2 Beat the egg yolks and whisk in a small amount of the hot chocolate sauce. Slowly pour the egg mixture into the saucepan, stirring rapidly. Cook over a low heat, stirring, for 10–15 minutes or until the mixture is very thick and creamy. Do not allow to boil. Remove from the heat.

3 Stir the butter and vanilla essence into the chocolate custard, then pour into the cold pastry case. Cover to prevent a skin forming and chill for about 4 hours or until set.

4 Just before serving, whip the cream lightly and spread evenly over the chocolate filling. Decorate the top with chocolate curls or grated chocolate. Serve chilled.

WHISKY MOCHA FLAN

This flan is made with a coffee-flavoured bavarois mixture and topped with whisky cream. We made ours in a heart-shaped tin.

SERVES 6–8

75 g (3 oz) plain chocolate
one 23 cm (9 inch) Pâte Sucrée
Tart Case (see page 84)

For the filling
10 ml (2 level tsp) powdered
gelatine
150 ml (¼ pint) milk
15 ml (1 level tbsp) instant coffee
granules
3 egg yolks
15 ml (1 level tbsp) caster sugar
150 ml (¼ pint) double cream

For the topping
200 ml (7 fl oz) double cream
15–30 ml (1–2 tbsp) whisky
15 ml (1 level tbsp) caster sugar
chocolate caraque (see page 13), to
decorate

1 Melt the chocolate (see page 12). Place the pastry case, upside-down, on a sheet of greaseproof paper. Using a pastry brush, brush half of the melted chocolate evenly all over the outside of the pastry case. Leave in a cool place until the chocolate sets. Turn the flan case over and brush the inside with the remaining chocolate. Leave in a cool place to set.

2 To make the filling, sprinkle the gelatine over 30 ml (2 tbsp) water in a small heat-proof bowl and leave to soak for 2–3 minutes. Place the bowl over a saucepan of simmering water and stir until the gelatine has dissolved.

3 Put the milk and coffee granules into a small saucepan. Heat gently until the coffee dissolves completely and the milk comes almost to the boil. Very lightly whisk the egg yolks and sugar together in a heatproof bowl. Pour in the coffee-flavoured milk and mix well.

4 Place the bowl over a pan of hot water and cook the custard, stirring continuously, until thick enough to coat the back of the spoon. As soon as the custard thickens, strain it through a nylon sieve into a clean bowl. Stir in the dissolved gelatine. Leave the custard to cool, stirring frequently to prevent a skin forming.

5 Whip the cream until it will just hold soft peaks, then gently fold it into the coffee custard. Place the chocolate-coated flan case on a flat serving plate and fill it with the coffee cream mixture. Chill until set.

6 To make the topping, whip the cream with the whisky and sugar until it will just hold soft peaks. Spread an even layer of cream over the top of the flan. Whip the remaining cream until thick enough to pipe and fill a piping bag fitted with a medium star nozzle. Pipe whirls of cream around the top of the flan, then decorate with chocolate caraque. Chill before serving.

CHOCOLATE MACAROON LOG

To make the hazelnut flavour more pronounced, substitute ground, unblanched hazelnuts for the almonds when making the macaroons, and omit the almond essence.

SERVES 10

For the macaroons
3 small egg whites (size 6)
175 g (6 oz) ground almonds
275 g (10 oz) caster sugar
7.5 ml (1½ tsp) almond essence

For the filling and decoration
125 g (4 oz) hazelnuts
125 g (4 oz) plain chocolate
300 ml (½ pint) double cream
*45 ml (3 tbsp) almond-flavoured
liqueur*
icing sugar for dusting
cocoa powder for dusting
chocolate leaves (see page 15)
hazelnuts

1 To make the macaroons, line two baking sheets with non-stick baking parchment. Whisk the egg whites until stiff, then fold in the almonds, sugar and almond essence.

2 Spoon the mixture into a piping bag fitted with a 1 cm (½ inch) plain nozzle and pipe 30 small rounds on to the prepared baking sheets, allowing room between each for the mixture to spread.

3 Bake in the oven at 180°C (350°F) mark 4 for about 20 minutes. Transfer to a wire rack and leave to cool for 20 minutes.

4 To make the filling, spread the nuts out on a baking sheet and brown them in the oven at 200°C (400°F) mark 6 for 5–10 minutes. Tip on to a tea-towel and rub off the skins. Chop finely.

5 Melt the chocolate (see page 12) and leave to cool for 5 minutes.

6 Whip the cream until it holds its shape. Gradually fold in the cooled chocolate, nuts and liqueur.

7 Use some of the chocolate cream to sandwich the macaroons together. Place them side by side on a serving plate to form a double log. Spread chocolate cream on top and add a further layer of macaroons. Spread the remaining chocolate cream over the top and sides of the macaroon log. Chill overnight in the refrigerator.

8 To serve, dust with icing sugar and cocoa powder, then decorate with chocolate leaves and whole hazelnuts.

CHOCOLATE AND CHESTNUT GINGER FLAN

SERVES 12

one 23 cm (9 inch) Pâte Sucrée
Tart Case (see page 84)

For the filling
50 g (2 oz) plain chocolate
75 ml (5 tbsp) stem ginger syrup
2 eggs
50 g (2 oz) caster sugar
150 ml (¼ pint) double or whipping
cream
425 g (15 oz) can unsweetened
chestnut purée
white and plain chocolate curls
(see page 15), to decorate

1 To make the filling, melt the chocolate with the ginger syrup (see page 12) and remove from the heat.

2 Whisk the eggs and sugar together in a bowl with an electric whisk, until very pale and thick. Whip the cream until it holds its shape and fold in the cool but not cold chocolate. Fold into the egg mixture.

3 Using an electric whisk, whip the chestnut purée with a quarter of the chocolate mixture until smooth. Gradually whisk in the remaining mixture. Cover and chill for at least 1 hour.

4 About 30 minutes before serving, spoon the mixture into the cold pastry case. Decorate with chocolate curls.

PETITS POTS DE CRÈME

If you do not have the special little china pots for making this rich cream, you can use small ramekin dishes. A less rich cream can be made by using milk instead of cream.

SERVES 6–8

600 ml (1 pint) single cream
2.5 ml (½ tsp) vanilla essence
225 g (8 oz) plain chocolate, broken
into small pieces
5 egg yolks, plus 1 whole egg
25 g (1 oz) caster sugar

1 Put the cream, vanilla essence and chocolate into a saucepan and heat gently, stirring, until the chocolate melts and the mixture is smooth.

2 Lightly mix together the egg yolks, whole egg and caster sugar, then stir in the chocolate cream. Strain the mixture through a nylon sieve into eight 75 ml (3 fl oz) petits pots, or six 125 ml (4 fl oz) ramekin dishes. Cover the petits pots or ramekins with lids or small rounds of foil.

3 Stand the dishes on a trivet in a large, wide saucepan, and add enough boiling water to come about halfway up the sides of the dishes. Cover the pan with a lid, then steam the creams over a very gentle heat for 15 minutes or until they are very lightly set and the centres are still slightly soft. Do not overcook or the smooth texture will be spoilt. Remove from the pan and allow to cool. Chill well before serving.

CHOCOLATE CINNAMON FLAN

Two-tone chocolate leaves make a stunning decoration for this flan which, when sliced, reveals its layers of creamy chocolate and cinnamon custard.

SERVES 6–8

1 quantity Shortcrust Pastry
(see page 108)

For the filling
300 ml (½ pint) milk
1 vanilla pod
15 ml (1 level tbsp) powdered
gelatine
3 eggs, separated
125 g (4 oz) caster sugar
50 g (2 oz) plain or milk chocolate
5 ml (1 level tsp) ground cinnamon

For the decoration
two-tone chocolate leaves
(see page 15)

1 Roll out the pastry very thinly and use to line a deep 24 cm (9½ inch) fluted flan ring on a baking sheet. Line with greaseproof paper or foil and weigh down with baking beans. Bake blind in the oven at 200°C (400°F) mark 6 for 20–25 minutes or until golden brown and cooked through. Remove the paper and beans and leave to cool.

2 To make the filling, put the milk and vanilla pod in a small saucepan and bring to the boil. Remove from the heat, cover and leave to infuse for about 30 minutes.

3 Sprinkle the gelatine over 45 ml (3 tbsp) water in a small heatproof bowl and leave to soak for 2–3 minutes. Place the bowl over a pan of simmering water and stir until dissolved.

4 Whisk the egg yolks and 75 g (3 oz) of the caster sugar together in a bowl until very pale and thick. Remove the vanilla pod from the milk. Return the milk to the boil and pour on to the egg mixture, whisking constantly.

5 Return the mixture to the pan and heat gently, without boiling, until it thickens enough to coat the back of a wooden spoon. Remove from the heat, add the dissolved gelatine and stir.

6 Divide the mixture between two bowls. Break the chocolate into one bowl and stir until melted. Cool until beginning to set. Whisk the cinnamon into the other bowl. Cool until beginning to set.

7 Whisk the egg whites until stiff but not dry. Add the remaining sugar and whisk again until stiff. Fold half the meringue mixture into each custard.

8 Pour half the chocolate custard into the pastry case. Freeze for a few minutes to set. Cover with the cinnamon custard and freeze quickly to set. Finish with the remaining chocolate mixture. Decorate with chocolate leaves and chill until ready to serve.

MOUSSE AND COLD SOUFFLÉ MAKING
YOUR PROBLEMS SOLVED

● Separate the eggs carefully. Just a trace of yolk in the egg white will make it almost impossible to whisk.

● Lightly whip the cream until it just holds its shape. Whisk the egg white until it forms soft peaks so that it can be mixed evenly into the mousse or soufflé. The trick is to get all the mixtures to a similar consistency so that they fold together quickly and evenly. Over-whisked egg whites make a lumpy, unevenly textured mousse.

● Similarly, aim to have all your ingredients at the same temperature; don't use cream straight from the refrigerator. If it is too cold, it will cause anything that's added to it (such as dissolved gelatine or melted chocolate) to set and harden.

● Dissolve soaked gelatine very gently; don't allow the water to boil furiously underneath the bowl. If it gets too hot and boils, it will not set.

● Always cool melted chocolate before adding it to a mousse or soufflé.

● Use a chocolate high in cocoa solids for the most intense flavour.

● If the mixture begins to set before the egg white is added, don't panic. Stand the bowl over a pan of gently simmering water until the warmth is sufficient to melt the mixture again. Don't let the mixture get too hot, and stir frequently, then cool again and complete as directed. The finished mousse or soufflé won't be quite as light and airy as it could be, but it will be perfectly acceptable.

● The young, the elderly, pregnant women and people with immune-deficiency diseases should not eat raw eggs due to the possible salmonella risk.

WHITE CHOCOLATE AND SHERRY MOUSSE

The chocolate horns can be made in advance. The filled horns will keep in the refrigerator for up to 2 days. Pack them in a single layer in a rigid container. Serve with a refreshing red fruit salad.

SERVES 8

125 g (4 oz) white chocolate
45 ml (3 tbsp) dry sherry or eau de
vie
150 ml (¼ pint) double cream
2 eggs, separated
5 ml (1 level tsp) powdered gelatine
15 ml (1 tbsp) milk
16 chocolate horns (see page 18), to
serve (optional)
chocolate shapes (see page 16), to
decorate

1 Melt the chocolate with the sherry and 30 ml (2 tbsp) water (see page 12). Stir well until the mixture is smooth, then beat in the egg yolks.
2 Lightly whip the cream until it just holds its shape. Fold in the chocolate mixture.
3 Sprinkle the gelatine over the milk in a small heatproof bowl and leave to soak for 2–3 minutes. Place the bowl over a pan of simmering water and stir until the gelatine has dissolved. Stir into the chocolate mixture. Chill until beginning to set.
4 Whisk the egg whites until stiff but not dry, then fold into the chocolate mixture. Leave to set until the consistency of whipped cream.
5 Stand the chocolate horns in tall glasses or mugs and spoon in the mousse. Alternatively, spoon the mousse directly into individual serving dishes. Chill for at least 1 hour before serving decorated with chocolate shapes.

CHOCOLATE AND LIME MOUSSE

Lime adds a refreshing tang to the chocolate flavour of this mousse.

SERVES 2

75 g (3 oz) plain chocolate
2 eggs, separated
15 ml (1 level tbsp) caster sugar
finely grated rind and strained juice
of 1 small lime
150 ml (¼ pint) double cream
2.5 ml (½ level tsp) powdered
gelatine
grated chocolate or twists of lime, to
decorate

1 Melt the chocolate (see page 12) and leave to cool slightly.
2 Whisk together the egg yolks, sugar and lime rind in a bowl, using an electric whisk, until thick and mousse-like. Whisk in the chocolate, then 30 ml (2 tbsp) of the cream.
3 Sprinkle the gelatine over the lime juice in a small heatproof bowl and leave to soak for 2–3 minutes. Place the bowl over a saucepan of simmering water and stir until the gelatine has dissolved. Whisk into the chocolate mixture.
4 Whisk the egg whites until stiff but not dry, then fold into the chocolate mixture.
5 Divide the mousse between two glasses and chill until set. Whip the remaining cream and use to decorate the desserts with grated chocolate or twists of lime. Leave at cool room temperature for about 30 minutes before serving.

CHOCOLATE MOUSSE CUPS

SERVES 6

*3 large sheets of filo pastry, each
measuring about 25.5 ×51 cm
(10 ×20 inches), thawed if frozen
25 g (1 oz) butter, melted
125 g (4 oz) plain chocolate
30 ml (2 tbsp) brandy
15 ml (1 level tbsp) instant coffee
powder
2 eggs, separated
150 ml (¼ pint) double cream
a few strawberries and icing sugar,
to decorate
Crème Anglaise (see page 154) and
strawberry purée, to serve (optional)*

1 Cut each filo pastry sheet into 12 squares. Line 12 deep bun tins with three overlapping squares, brushing with melted butter between each layer.
2 Bake blind in the oven at 200°C (400°F) mark 6 for 10–12 minutes or until the pastry is crisp, golden brown and cooked through. Turn out on to a wire rack and leave to cool.
3 Break the chocolate into small pieces and put it in a heatproof bowl with the brandy, coffee powder and 15 ml (1 tbsp) water. Stand the bowl over a pan of simmering water and heat gently until the chocolate melts. Stir the mixture until smooth.
4 Stir the egg yolks into the chocolate mixture and leave to cool slightly. Lightly whip the cream and fold it into the chocolate mixture. Whisk the egg whites until stiff but not dry, then fold into the chocolate mixture. Leave to set until the consistency of thick cream. Spoon the mousse into the pastry cups and chill for 1 hour.
5 Decorate each cup with a few strawberries and dust heavily with icing sugar before serving with crème anglaise and a little strawberry purée, if liked.

CHOCOLATE AND ORANGE TRIFLE

Use bought chocolate cake or use up home-made cake that's past its best.

SERVES 8

*350 g (12 oz) chocolate sponge
cake
4 large, juicy oranges
120 ml (8 tbsp) orange-flavoured
liqueur
4 egg yolks
50 g (2 oz) caster sugar
45 ml (3 level tbsp) cornflour
a few drops of vanilla essence
568 ml (1 pint) milk
45 ml (3 tbsp) stem ginger syrup
300 ml (½ pint) double cream
toasted almonds and stem ginger,
to decorate*

1 Thinly slice the cake and use it to line the base of a shallow serving dish.
2 Peel and segment the oranges. Arrange the segments on top of the cake. Spoon the liqueur evenly over the cake and orange.
3 In a heavy-based, preferably non-stick, saucepan, combine the egg yolks, sugar, cornflour and vanilla essence. Gradually stir in the milk and ginger syrup. Bring the mixture almost to the boil and simmer for 4–5 minutes or until thickened, stirring all the time.
4 Pour the custard evenly into the dish and leave to cool.
5 Whip the cream until it just holds its shape, then spoon on top of the custard. Decorate with almonds and stem ginger.

Opposite: Chocolate Mousse Cups

DARK AND LIGHT CHOCOLATE TERRINE

A wickedly delicious chocoholic's dream! Be careful when slicing, as the terrine softens very quickly.

SERVES 6–8

For the praline
225 g (8 oz) blanched almonds or skinned hazelnuts
125 g (4 oz) granulated sugar

For the dark chocolate mousse
175 g (6 oz) plain chocolate
75 g (3 oz) unsalted butter, softened
75 g (3 oz) caster sugar
30 ml (2 tbsp) cocoa powder, sifted
3 egg yolks
30 ml (2 tbsp) rum or brandy
300 ml (½ pint) double or whipping cream

For the white chocolate mousse
175 g (6 oz) white chocolate
50 g (2 oz) unsalted butter, softened
2 egg yolks
200 ml (7 fl oz) double or whipping cream

1 Grease a 750 ml (1¼ pint) loaf tin and line it with cling film. Lightly oil a baking sheet.

2 To make the praline, toast the nuts in the oven at 180°C (350°F) mark 4 until golden brown, stirring occasionally. Put the sugar in a heavy-based saucepan with 15 ml (1 tbsp) water. Heat gently until the sugar has dissolved, then stir in the warm nuts and boil until the syrup starts to brown. Immediately pour on to the prepared baking sheet. Leave to cool completely, then roughly crush with a rolling pin or in a blender or food processor. Store in an airtight tin until needed.

3 To make the mousses, melt both chocolates in separate bowls (see page 12). Stir until smooth, then leave to cool slightly.

4 To make the dark chocolate mousse, cream the butter and half the sugar together until pale and creamy. Beat in the cocoa powder. In another bowl, beat the egg yolks and the remaining sugar together until pale. Stir in the rum. Whip the cream until it just holds its shape. Working quickly, beat the melted plain chocolate into the creamed butter. Stir this into the yolk mixture, then carefully fold in the cream. Set aside.

5 To make the white chocolate mousse, beat the butter into the melted white chocolate. Stir in the egg yolks and 30 ml (2 tbsp) crushed praline. Whip the cream until it just holds its shape and fold into the chocolate mixture.

6 Drop large spoonfuls of each mousse alternately into the prepared tin until full. Tap the tin on the work surface to level the mixture. Cover and chill for at least 4 hours (preferably overnight) until very firm.

7 To serve, turn the mousse out on to a flat serving dish and peel off the cling film. With a palette knife, press the remaining praline over the top and sides of the terrine. Chill for 30 minutes to firm, then serve cut into slices. This dessert is so rich it needs nothing extra to accompany it.

CHOCOLATE ORANGE SOUFFLÉ

SERVES 6–8

450 ml (¾ pint) milk
150 g (5 oz) plain chocolate
3 eggs, separated, plus 1 egg white
75 g (3 oz) sugar
15 ml (1 level tbsp) powdered gelatine
grated rind and juice of 1 orange
300 ml (½ pint) whipping cream
15 ml (1 tbsp) chocolate-flavoured liqueur
grated chocolate, to decorate

1 Tie a double strip of greaseproof paper around a 900 ml (1½ pint) soufflé dish to make a 7.5 cm (3 inch) collar. Lightly brush the inside of the paper with oil.

2 Put the milk in a saucepan and add the chocolate. Heat gently until the chocolate melts, then bring almost to the boil.

3 Whisk the egg yolks and sugar together in a bowl until pale and thick. Gradually pour on the chocolate milk, stirring. Return to the pan and cook gently, without boiling, for about 20 minutes, stirring, until the mixture coats the back of a wooden spoon.

4 Sprinkle the gelatine over 45 ml (3 tbsp) water in a small heatproof bowl and leave to soak for 2–3 minutes. Place the bowl over simmering water and stir until the gelatine dissolves. Stir into the custard with the orange rind and juice. Cool.

5 Whip the cream until it just holds its shape, then fold most of the cream into the cold mixture. Whisk the egg whites until stiff, then fold into the mixture.

6 Pour the soufflé mixture into the prepared dish and leave to set. Carefully ease away the paper collar just before serving.

7 Stir the liqueur into the remaining cream and use to decorate the soufflé. Sprinkle the top with grated chocolate.

CHOCOLATE LACE BASKETS

These dainty lace baskets are made with Chocolate Flavour Cake Covering. When set, it is less brittle than plain chocolate and is therefore less likely to crack. Don't attempt these unless you have time to spare, as they require patience.

SERVES 6

150 g (5 oz) plain Chocolate Flavour Cake Covering
1 small mango
¼ fresh pineapple
12 strawberries
1 passion fruit
whipped cream, to serve

1 Melt the Chocolate Flavour Cake Covering (see page 12).

2 Invert six 8.5 cm (3½ inch) ring moulds and stretch cling film over the rounded bases to cover completely.

3 Spoon half the melted chocolate cake covering into a greaseproof paper piping bag and snip off the point. Pipe three of the ring moulds with a lacy pattern of cake covering.

4 Fill a second bag with melted cake covering and pipe the remaining three moulds. Chill until set.

5 Meanwhile, peel the mango and chop the flesh, discarding the stone. Cut the pineapple flesh into pieces. Hull the strawberries. Halve the passion fruit and scoop out the pulp.

6 Carefully lift the chocolate baskets with the cling film, then remove the cling film from the shells. Fill the baskets with the fruit and serve with whipped cream.

CHOCOLATE AND NUT-FILLED FIGS

Although this recipe uses no-soak figs, as they're easier to fill, we still recommend soaking them.

SERVES 6

350 g (12 oz) no-soak dried figs
90 ml (6 tbsp) orange-flavoured
liqueur, such as Cointreau or Grand
Marnier
150 ml (¼ pint) water
25 g (1 oz) pistachio nuts
25 g (1 oz) walnut halves
75 g (3 oz) plain chocolate, broken
into pieces
walnut halves, to decorate
(optional)
a mixture of natural yogurt and
cream, to serve

1 Place the figs in a bowl and pour over the liqueur and water. Cover and leave to soak for about 3 hours.
2 Skin the pistachio nuts and put them in a food processor with the walnut halves and chocolate. Add 45 ml (3 tbsp) of the soaking juices and blend until roughly chopped.
3 Make a small hole in the stem end of each fig and use a teaspoon to fill with the stuffing. Close over the hole and top with a walnut half, if wished.
4 Place the figs, side by side, in an oven-proof dish and spoon over the remaining soaking juices. Serve cold with natural yogurt and cream.

CARAMEL MOUSSE

This is a rich, easily made mousse, best left in the refrigerator overnight.

SERVES 6

three 61.5 g Mars bars
15 ml (1 tbsp) milk
300 ml (½ pint) double cream
1 egg white

For the decoration
caster sugar
whipped cream
cape gooseberries

1 Thinly slice the Mars bars and put them in a heatproof bowl with the milk. Place over a saucepan of simmering water, and heat gently, stirring occasionally, until melted and almost smooth. Cool for about 10 minutes, stirring occasionally.
2 Whip the cream until it just holds its shape, then gently stir a large spoonful into the Mars bar mixture. Fold in the remaining cream with a large metal spoon.
3 Lightly whisk the egg white and fold it into the chocolate mixture. Pour into a bowl, cover and leave in the refrigerator over-night.
4 To make crushed caramel to decorate, line a small baking sheet with foil and brush generously with oil. Sprinkle caster sugar evenly over the foil and cook under a hot grill until melted and golden. (Don't take your eyes off it for a second as it can suddenly catch and burn.) As the sugar melts it will run into uneven pools of caramel. Remove from the grill immediately and allow to cool slightly before peeling off the foil and breaking into pieces. Use to decorate the mousse with the whipped cream and cape gooseberries.

Opposite: Caramel Mousse

DOUBLE CHOCOLATE SOUFFLÉ

To serve this soufflé in a case, use a warm knife to cut it into wedge-shaped pieces. It's very rich but very good too! The finished, decorated soufflé can be frozen and simply thawed overnight when required.

SERVES 8

400 g (14 oz) plain chocolate
200 ml (7 fl oz) double cream
30 ml (2 tbsp) brandy, rum or
Kahlua
10 ml (2 level tsp) powdered
gelatine
3 eggs, separated
50 g (2 oz) caster sugar
white, milk and plain chocolate
curls (see page 13), to decorate
cocoa powder for dusting

1 Lightly grease a 21.5 cm (8½ inch) moule à manqué tin and line the base and sides with non-stick baking parchment, keeping the sides as smooth as possible. Stand the mould on a baking sheet.
2 Melt half the chocolate (see page 12) and leave to cool slightly.
3 Spoon the chocolate into the centre of the mould. Gently tip and brush it up the sides of the mould to coat the base and sides of the tin evenly (a pastry brush will help). Freeze for about 1 hour or until firm. Carefully ease off the tin and gently peel away the non-stick baking parchment. Place the chocolate case on a baking sheet in the refrigerator.
4 Melt the remaining chocolate with 45 ml (3 tbsp) of the cream and the brandy. Leave the mixture to cool slightly.
5 Sprinkle the gelatine over 30 ml (2 tbsp) water in a small heatproof bowl and leave to soak for 2–3 minutes. Place the bowl over a saucepan of simmering water and stir until the gelatine has dissolved.
6 Whisk the egg yolks with the sugar until thick and mousse-like. Stir in the dissolved gelatine and the cooled chocolate mixture. Lightly whip the remaining cream and fold it in.
7 Whisk the egg whites until they form soft peaks and fold into the chocolate mixture. Pour gently into the chocolate case. Refrigerate for about 3 hours or until set.
8 Decorate the soufflé with chocolate curls and leave at room temperature for 10–15 minutes to soften slightly before serving. Dust the top of the soufflé with cocoa powder to serve.

CHOCOLATE SNOWBALL

This luscious dessert must be left for at least 24 hours before eating. The outer layer forms a crust while the centre remains soft and fudge-like.

SERVES 4–6

175 g (6 oz) plain chocolate
7.5 ml (1½ level tsp) instant coffee
granules
175 g (6 oz) caster sugar
175 g (6 oz) unsalted butter, diced
4 eggs
15 ml (1 tbsp) dark rum
225 ml (8 fl oz) double cream
frosted petals, to decorate (optional)

1 Line a 750 ml (1¼ pint) pudding basin with foil.
2 Melt the chocolate in a large heatproof bowl (see page 12). Dissolve the coffee in 45 ml (3 tbsp) water and add it to the bowl with the sugar. Heat gently until the sugar dissolves, then remove from the heat.
3 Whisk the chocolate mixture thoroughly with an electric hand-held mixer or a balloon whisk. Slowly whisk in the butter until evenly combined. Whisk in the eggs, one at a time. Stir in the rum. Pour the mixture into the prepared pudding basin.
4 Bake in the oven at 180°C (350°F) mark 4 for about 1¼ hours or until risen and firm, but still slightly wobbly, like a soufflé, with a thick, cracked crust.
5 Leave to cool at room temperature, then press down to level the surface. Cover and chill for at least 24 hours.
6 Unmould the dessert on to a serving plate and peel off the foil. Whip the cream until it holds its shape. Spoon the cream into a piping bag fitted with a star nozzle and pipe rosettes on the pudding until completely covered. Decorate with a sprinkling of frosted petals, if wished.

MISSISSIPPI MUD PIE

This is a simpler version of the Frozen Mississippi Mud Pie on page 116. Serve warm with Chocolate Fudge Sauce (see page 153) or ice cream, or cold with whipped cream.

SERVES 16

For the base
150 g (5 oz) ginger biscuits,
crushed
150 g (5 oz) digestive biscuits,
crushed
125 g (4 oz) butter, melted

For the filling
225 g (8 oz) butter or margarine
175 g (6 oz) plain chocolate, broken
into pieces
120 ml (8 level tbsp) golden syrup
4 eggs, beaten
50 g (2 oz) pecan nuts, chopped

1 Grease a 23 cm (9 inch) loose-based cake tin.
2 To make the base, mix the biscuits with the butter. Press into the bottom and 4 cm (1½ inches) up the sides of the prepared tin. Chill while making the filling.
3 To make the filling, put the butter, chocolate and syrup in a saucepan and heat very gently until melted, stirring all the time. Cool, then beat in the eggs and pecans. Pour the mixture into the biscuit crust.
4 Bake in the oven at 180°C (350°F) mark 4 for 1¼ hours or until just firm to the touch but still soft in the centre. Serve warm or cold with chocolate sauce, ice cream or whipped cream.

Chocolate Heaven

There are numerous versions of this wickedly rich concoction, but most are based on liquid glucose, which can be difficult to find in the shops. This recipe uses golden syrup instead – it's easier to obtain and gives an excellent result.

SERVES ABOUT 12

75 g (3 oz) shelled hazelnuts
450 g (1 lb) couverture or plain chocolate, chopped
60 ml (4 tbsp) brandy or orange-flavoured liqueur, or liqueur of your choice
75 ml (5 tbsp) golden syrup
600 ml (1 pint) double cream
cocoa powder and chocolate wattles (see page 20), to decorate

1 Oil a 25.5 cm (10 inch) spring-release cake tin. Line the base with greaseproof paper and oil the paper.
2 Brown the hazelnuts under a hot grill, shaking the grill pan occasionally so that they brown on all sides. Tip into a clean tea-towel and rub off the skins. Grill again until thoroughly toasted, being careful not to let them burn. Cool, then put them in a food processor and chop them very finely. Sprinkle the finely chopped nuts evenly in the base of the prepared tin.
3 Put the chocolate, liqueur and golden syrup in a large bowl. Stand the bowl over a pan of simmering water and stir until the chocolate has melted. Remove the bowl from the saucepan and leave to cool slightly.
4 Lightly whip the cream until it *just* holds its shape. (Do not over-whip or the texture of the finished dessert will be ruined.) Fold a quarter of the cream into the chocolate mixture, then fold in the remainder. Carefully pour into the prepared tin on top of the nuts. Tap the tin on the work surface once or twice to release any air bubbles. Cover with cling film, then chill in the refrigerator for several hours, preferably overnight, or until set.
5 To serve, carefully loosen the dessert from the sides of the tin with a palette knife, then release the sides of the tin. Lift out on to a plate so that the nuts are still underneath. Dredge thickly with cocoa powder and decorate with chocolate waffles before serving.

CHOCOLATE BAVAROIS

SERVES 8

bland oil, such as sunflower
900 ml (1½ pints) milk, or milk and
single cream mixed
1 vanilla pod, split, or a few drops
of vanilla essence
125 g (4 oz) plain chocolate,
chopped
6 egg yolks (size 2)
50 g (2 oz) caster sugar
20 ml (4 level tsp) powdered
gelatine
300 ml (½ pint) double cream
mixture of summer fruits (such as
strawberries, redcurrants and
blueberries) and sweet herbs (such
as mint, chervil and dill),
to decorate

For the fruit purée
225 g (8 oz) blackcurrants, stalks
removed
225 g (8 oz) raspberries
75 g (3 oz) caster sugar

1 Lightly oil a 1.4 litre (2½ pint) ring mould or a deep 1.4 litre (2½ pint) cake tin or glass dish. Turn the mould upside-down on a piece of absorbent kitchen paper to allow any excess oil to drain off.

2 Put the milk in a saucepan with the vanilla pod, if using, and the chocolate. Heat gently until the chocolate has melted, then remove from the heat. Cover and leave to infuse for 30 minutes.

3 Meanwhile, beat the egg yolks with the sugar until thick and almost white. Strain the milk on to the egg and sugar mixture and stir well until evenly blended. Add the vanilla essence, if using.

4 Rinse the saucepan, then pour the custard mixture back into the pan and cook very gently for 10–12 minutes, stirring all the time with a wooden spoon until it thick-ens enough to coat the back of the spoon. Do not allow the mixture to boil or it will curdle. Don't rush this stage or the velvety texture of the custard will be lost. Strain into a large bowl, cover the surface with damp greaseproof paper and set aside to cool at room temperature.

5 Sprinkle the gelatine over 60 ml (4 tbsp) water in a small heatproof bowl and leave to soak for 2–3 minutes. Stand the bowl over a pan of simmering water and stir until the gelatine has dissolved.

6 Remove the greaseproof paper from the cooled (but not cold) custard. Pour in the liquid gelatine, stirring well. Place the bowl in a roasting tin of water and surround with ice to speed up the process of thickening/setting. Stir constantly for about 15 minutes or until the custard begins to resemble lightly whipped cream. Remove from the ice.

7 Working quickly, whip the cream until *just* beginning to thicken, then lightly fold into the custard with a large metal spoon. The trick is to get the cream to the same consistency as the custard. If too thick, it won't fold in evenly and will form small lumps through the mixture. If it is too thin, the custard will not hold any air and may become rather solid.

8 Pour the custard into the prepared mould and chill in the refrigerator for at least 4 hours or until set. Make sure that the refrigerator shelf is level or the finished Bavarois will be lop-sided. Allow 4½–5 hours for the Bavarois to set if using a deep cake tin or glass dish.

9 Meanwhile, place the blackcurrants and raspberries in a saucepan with the caster sugar and 300 ml (½ pint) water. Heat gently until the sugar dissolves, then bring to the boil. Cover and simmer for 10 minutes or until the fruits are very soft. Cool, then purée the contents of the pan in a blender or food processor. Sieve into a bowl. Cover and store in the refrigerator.

10 To turn out the Bavarois, gently ease

the edges of the custard away from the tin with a dampened finger. This breaks the air-lock. Moisten a flat plate and place it upside-down over the tin. Invert the plate and tin and give a series of gentle shakes sideways and down until the Bavarois loosens. Carefully ease off the tin and slide the custard into the centre of the plate. Bring to room temperature about 30 minutes–1 hour before serving. Moisten some of the mixed fruit with one or two spoonfuls of fruit purée, then spoon into the centre of the Bavarois. Pour a little of the purée around the custard and decorate with fruit and fresh herbs. Serve the remaining purée separately.

CRANBERRY CREAMS

SERVES 8

*225 g (8 oz) fresh or frozen
cranberries*
125 g (4 oz) caster sugar
30 ml (2 tbsp) port
*20 ml (4 level tsp) powdered
gelatine*
*45 ml (3 tbsp) lemon juice,
strained, or kirsch*
175 g (6 oz) white chocolate
300 ml (½ pint) single cream
6 egg yolks
300 ml (½ pint) double cream
*grated white chocolate or white
chocolate leaves (see page 15), to
decorate*

1 Lightly oil eight 150 ml (¼ pint) ramekin dishes. Line the bases and sides of the dishes with non-stick baking parchment.
2 Put the cranberries in a small saucepan with 75 g (3 oz) of the sugar, the port and 300 ml (½ pint) water. Bring to the boil, cover and simmer gently for 10 minutes or until the cranberries begin to soften. Strain

the mixture, reserving both the liquid and berries.
3 Sprinkle 5 ml (1 level tsp) gelatine over 200 ml (7 fl oz) of the reserved cranberry liquid in a heatproof bowl. (Return the remainder of the liquid to the reserved berries.) Leave to soak for 2–3 minutes. Place the bowl over a saucepan of simmering water and stir until the gelatine has dissolved. Allow to cool and thicken slightly. Spoon into the prepared ramekin dishes and refrigerate until set.
4 Sprinkle the remaining gelatine over the lemon juice or kirsch in a heatproof bowl. Leave to soak.
5 Melt the chocolate with the single cream (see page 12). Stir until smooth.
6 Lightly whisk the egg yolks with the remaining sugar. Pour in the chocolate mixture, whisking continuously. Return to the bowl and continue to heat the mixture over the simmering water until thick enough to coat the back of a wooden spoon.
7 Add the gelatine and stir until completely dissolved, then leave to cool. Lightly whip the double cream and fold into the mixture. Divide between the ramekin dishes and return to the refrigerator to set.
8 To unmould the cranberry creams, place an individual serving plate upside-down on top of each ramekin and invert. Remove the lining paper. Decorate the creams with the reserved cranberry mixture and grated white chocolate or white chocolate leaves.

ZUCCOTTO

SERVES 6

45 ml (3 tbsp) brandy
30 ml (2 tbsp) orange-flavoured
liqueur
30 ml (2 tbsp) cherry- or almond-
flavoured liqueur
350 g (12 oz) trifle sponges or
Madeira cake
150 g (5 oz) bittersweet or plain
chocolate
450 ml (¾ pint) double cream
125 g (4 oz) icing sugar
50 g (2 oz) blanched almonds,
toasted and chopped
50 g (2 oz) hazelnuts, toasted and
chopped
icing sugar and cocoa powder, to
decorate

1 Line a 1.4 litre (2½ pint) pudding basin or round-bottomed bowl with damp muslin. In a separate bowl, mix together the brandy and liqueurs and set aside.

2 Split the trifle sponges in half through the centre (if using Madeira cake, cut into 1 cm/ ½ inch slices). Sprinkle with the brandy and liqueurs. Line the basin with the moistened sponges, reserving enough to cover the top.

3 Using a sharp knife, chop 75 g (3 oz) of the chocolate into small pieces and set aside. Whip the cream and icing sugar together until stiff, then fold in the chopped chocolate and nuts.

4 Divide this mixture in two and spread one half over the sponge lining in an even layer.

5 Melt the remaining chocolate (see page 12). Cool slightly, then fold into the remaining cream mixture. Use this to fill the centre of the pudding.

6 Level the top of the Zuccotto and cover with remaining moistened sponge. Trim the edges. Cover and chill for at least 12 hours.

7 To serve, uncover the Zuccotto and invert a flat serving plate over the top of it. Turn upside-down, lift off the bowl and carefully remove the muslin. Serve cold, dusted with icing sugar and cocoa powder.

ALMOND AND HONEY WAFERS

The chocolate is surprisingly easy to pipe. Don't worry if the lattices are rough and irregular; they look better that way!

SERVES 6

150 g (5 oz) plain chocolate
125 g (4 oz) white Toblerone
75 ml (5 level tbsp) double cream
about 150 ml (¼ pint) soured cream
icing sugar for dusting
cape gooseberries, to serve

1 Line baking sheets with non-stick baking parchment. Melt the plain chocolate (see page 12) and leave to cool slightly. Spoon half the chocolate at a time into a small paper piping bag fitted with a fine icing nozzle.

2 Pipe thin lines of chocolate to form about 12 rough lattice shapes about 7.5 cm (3 inches) in diameter. Refrigerate to set.

3 Meanwhile, break the Toblerone into a bowl and add the double cream. Place over a pan of gently simmering water until the chocolate melts, then stir well to combine. (The mixture will not be completely smooth as there are chopped almonds in Toblerone bars.) Leave to cool. Mix in the soured cream, cover and refrigerate.

4 To serve, peel the lattices off the lining paper and sandwich carefully with the Toblerone mixture. Keep chilled until serving time. Dust lightly with icing sugar to decorate. Serve with cape gooseberries.

CHAPTER FIVE

FROZEN DESSERTS

HOME-MADE ICE CREAM
YOUR PROBLEMS SOLVED

There is nothing to beat the rich flavour and creamy texture of home-made ice cream.

The knack of successfully achieving a smooth result largely depends on making sure that no large ice crystals form during freezing. This means that it is necessary to whisk the freezing mixture periodically by hand, if you do not own an ice cream machine, which will do the job for you.

Ice cream can be stored in the freezer for up to 3 months.

To Freeze Ice Cream By Hand
The following freezing times based on 900 ml (1½ pints) ice cream are given as a guide. If making a larger quantity of ice cream, the times should be increased.

1 Set the freezer to maximum or 'fast freeze' about 1 hour before you intend to freeze the mixture.
2 Make the ice cream as directed in the recipe.
3 Pour the mixture into a shallow, non-metallic freezer container. Cover and freeze for about 3 hours or until just frozen all over but still with a mushy consistency.
4 Spoon into a bowl and mash with a fork or flat whisk to break down the ice crystals. Work quickly so that the ice cream does not melt completely.
5 Return the mixture to the shallow container and freeze again for about 2 hours.
6 Mash again as described in step 4. If any other ingredients are to be added, such as nuts or chocolate drops, then fold them in at this stage.
7 Return to the freezer and freeze for about 3 hours or until firm.

8 Remove from the freezer and leave at room temperature for 20–30 minutes to soften before serving. (Do not forget to return the freezer setting to normal.)

Ice Cream Machines
An ice cream machine will freeze an ice cream mixture and churn it at the same time, thus eliminating the physical effort. The results will be smooth and even-textured.

There are several types of ice cream machine available. Some use a salt solution and others a disc which needs to be frozen before use. Always follow manufacturer's instructions.

Generally speaking, the cooled mixture should be poured into the machine when the paddles are moving, otherwise it tends to freeze on to the base and sides of the bowl, stopping the paddles working. When making ice cream this way, if the recipe calls for whipped cream, it should be ignored. The cream can simply be added from the carton with the custard.

Freezing time is usually about 20–30 minutes. The ice cream should then be transferred to the freezer and frozen for 1–2 hours to allow the flavours to develop before serving. Soften slightly at room temperature before serving.

It is vital to clean ice cream machines thoroughly after using to prevent development of bacteria. Wash bowls, lids, paddles and spatulas in the hottest water temperature possible. Be sure to wash and dry all parts which come into contact with salt to prevent corrosion.

DOUBLE CHOCOLATE ICE CREAM

SERVES 4–6

1 vanilla pod or 1.25 ml (¼ tsp)
vanilla essence
300 ml (½ pint) milk
125 g (4 oz) plain chocolate, broken
into pieces
3 egg yolks
50–75 g (2–3 oz) caster sugar
300 ml (½ pint) double cream
50 g (2 oz) plain chocolate drops

1 Split the vanilla pod, if using, to reveal the seeds. Put the milk, vanilla pod and plain chocolate in a heavy-based saucepan and heat gently until the chocolate has melted. Increase the heat and bring almost to the boil. Remove from the heat, cover and leave to infuse for about 20 minutes.

2 Beat the egg yolks and sugar together in a bowl until well blended. Stir in the milk and strain back into the pan. Cook the custard over a gentle heat, stirring all the time, until it thickens very slightly. It is very important not to let the custard boil or it will curdle. Pour out into a bowl and leave to cool.

3 Whisk the cream into the cold custard mixture, with the vanilla essence, if using.

4 Freeze the mixture in an ice cream machine or by hand to the end of step 5 (see page 112). Mash again, then stir in the chocolate drops. Freeze until firm. Leave at cool room temperature for 20–30 minutes to soften before serving.

BITTER CHOCOLATE AND LIQUEUR ICE CREAM

SERVES 4–6

300 ml (½ pint) milk
125 g (4 oz) bittersweet chocolate,
broken into pieces
30 ml (2 tbsp) orange-flavoured
liqueur
3 egg yolks
50–75 g (2–3 oz) caster sugar
300 ml (½ pint) double cream

1 Put the milk in a heavy-based saucepan and bring almost to the boil. Meanwhile, melt the chocolate with the liqueur (see page 12).

2 Beat the egg yolks and sugar together until well blended. Stir in the milk and strain back into the pan. Cook the custard over a gentle heat, stirring all the time, until it thickens very slightly. It is very important not to let the custard boil or it will curdle. Remove the custard from the heat, stir in the melted chocolate until evenly blended, then pour out into a bowl and leave to cool.

3 Whisk the cream into the cold custard mixture. Freeze the mixture by hand or in an ice cream machine (see page 112). Leave at cool room temperature for 20–30 minutes to soften before serving.

CHOCOLATE FLAKE ICE CREAM

SERVES 4–6

1 vanilla pod or 1.25 ml (¼ tsp)
vanilla essence
300 ml (½ pint) milk
3 egg yolks
50–75 g (2–3 oz) caster sugar
300 ml (½ pint) double cream
2 large chocolate flakes, crumbled

1 Split the vanilla pod, if using, to reveal the seeds. Put the milk and vanilla pod in a heavy-based saucepan and bring almost to the boil. Remove from the heat, cover and leave to infuse for about 20 minutes.
2 Beat the egg yolks and sugar together until well blended. Stir in the milk and strain back into the pan. Cook the custard over a gentle heat, stirring all the time, until it thickens very slightly. It is very important not to let the custard boil or it will curdle. Pour out into a bowl and leave to cool.
3 Whisk the cream into the cold custard mixture, with the vanilla essence, if using, and half of the crumbled flake.
4 Freeze the mixture by hand or in an ice cream machine (see page 112), folding in the remaining flake just before the ice cream is completely frozen. Leave at cool room temperature for 20–30 minutes to soften before serving.

FROZEN CHOCOLATE TERRINE WITH BRANDIED PRUNES

SERVES 14

225 g (8 oz) no-soak stoned dried
prunes
150 ml (¼ pint) cold tea
45 ml (3 tbsp) brandy
225 g (8 oz) plain chocolate
4 eggs, separated
75 g (3 oz) icing sugar, sifted
25 g (1 oz) cocoa powder, sifted
300 ml (½ pint) double cream

1 Put the prunes, tea and brandy in a bowl and leave to soak for 3–4 hours or overnight. Drain, reserving the liquid, then roughly chop the prunes.
2 Melt the chocolate (see page 12), then leave to cool slightly.
3 Using an electric whisk, whisk the egg whites and icing sugar together in a bowl to make a stiff meringue. Fold in the cocoa powder.
4 Whip the double cream until it just holds soft peaks. Whisk the egg yolks until pale and fluffy, then whisk in the chocolate.
5 Carefully fold the egg yolk and chocolate mixture into the meringue, followed by the cream. Fold in the soaked prunes and the reserved liquid.
6 Pour the mixture into a 1.1 litre (2 pint) terrine. Cover and freeze for at least 5 hours or until firm.
7 To serve, dip the terrine briefly in hot water, then turn out on to a serving plate. Serve cut into slices with single cream.

Opposite: Frozen Terrine with Brandied Prunes; Chocolate Nut Snaps (page 140)

ICED BLACK FOREST GÂTEAU

The sponge quickly softens to give a delicious base for this gâteau.

SERVES **8**

2 eggs
75 g (3 oz) caster sugar
50 g (2 oz) plain flour
25 g (1 oz) cocoa powder, sifted

For the filling and decoration
454 g (16 oz) can stoned cherries
30 ml (2 tbsp) kirsch
600 ml (1 pint) tub soft-scoop
vanilla ice cream
40 g (1½ oz) toasted flaked
almonds
chocolate curls (see page 13)

1 Grease a 20.5 cm (8 inch) round cake tin and line the base with greaseproof paper. Dust with a little caster sugar and flour.
2 Using an electric whisk, beat the eggs and caster sugar together until pale and thick. Gently fold in the flour and cocoa powder, and spoon into the prepared tin.
3 Bake in the oven at 180°C (350°F) mark 4 for about 30 minutes or until firm to the touch. Turn out on to a wire rack and leave to cool.
4 To make the filling, drain the cherries, reserving the juice. Mix 90 ml (6 tbsp) juice with the kirsch. Finely chop the cherries.
5 Cut the cake horizontally into two layers and place the base on a flat plate. Spoon on half the kirsch and juice, and all the cherries. Top with spoonfuls of ice cream, then the second layer of cake and remaining juices. Sprinkle with flaked almonds and chocolate curls.
6 Place immediately in the freezer and freeze for at least 3 hours. Overwrap once firm. Leave at cool room temperature for about 40 minutes to soften before serving cut into wedges.

FROZEN MISSISSIPPI MUD PIE

The origin of Mississippi Mud Pie is rather vague; our research led us to some unusual recipes and unlikely tales. According to one story, the recipe originated on the banks of the Mississippi River, where the coffee-coloured clay was baked into small edible pies – hence the name. Many American recipes used ice cream to make the pie. We tried our version in the freezer and discovered it tasted wonderful, so we recommend serving it as a frozen dessert.

SERVES 16

For the base
50 g (2 oz) butter
75 g (3 oz) digestive biscuits
75 g (3 oz) ginger biscuits

For the filling
600 ml (1 pint) double cream
450 g (1 lb) caster sugar
60 ml (4 level tbsp) cornflour
4 eggs (size 1)
125 g (4 oz) butter, diced
5 ml (1 tsp) vanilla essence
30 ml (2 tbsp) rum
10 ml (2 tsp) chicory and coffee
essence

For the topping and decoration
125 g (4 oz) plain chocolate
2 eggs (size 1), separated
150 ml (¼ pint) double cream
icing sugar and cocoa powder for
dusting
chocolate curls (see page 13)

1 To make the base, lightly oil a deep 20.5 cm (8 inch) spring-release cake tin and line the base and sides with non-stick baking parchment. Melt the butter, then leave to cool slightly. Finely crush all the biscuits either by placing them in a strong bag and crushing them with a rolling pin or by blending in a food processor. Add to the butter and stir until evenly combined. Press the biscuit mixture evenly over the base of the prepared tin. Chill in the refrigerator for about 30 minutes or until firm.

2 To make the filling, put the cream and sugar in a heavy-based non-stick saucepan and heat very gently, stirring occasionally, until the sugar has completely dissolved. Remove from the heat. Mix the cornflour to a smooth paste with 60 ml (4 tbsp) cold water. Lightly beat the eggs.

3 Stir the cornflour and beaten eggs into the cream and sugar mixture and beat well until thoroughly combined and smooth. Return the mixture to the heat and slowly bring to the boil, stirring constantly with a wooden spoon, until the mixture becomes very thick and smooth, like fudge. This will take 15–20 minutes.

4 Beat the butter into the fudge mixture, one piece at a time, with all the remaining filling ingredients, until well combined and the mixture is very smooth and creamy once more.

5 Pour the filling over the chilled biscuit base. Allow to cool completely, then place in the freezer for at least 1 hour, preferably overnight, to set.

6 For the topping, melt the chocolate (see page 12). Whisk the egg yolks and cream together until well blended.

7 Add the cream mixture to the melted chocolate and whisk until smooth. Place in a small, heavy-based saucepan over a low heat and stir constantly for about 10 minutes or until the mixture is smooth and thickly coats the back of a wooden spoon. Do not boil or the mixture will curdle. Remove from the heat and leave to cool completely. Press a damp piece of greaseproof paper gently on to the surface to prevent a skin forming.

8 When the chocolate mixture is cool, lightly whisk the egg whites until they just hold soft peaks. Stir about one third into the chocolate mixture, then gently fold in the remainder.

9 Pour the chocolate mixture evenly over the set fudge filling, levelling the surface if necessary with a round-bladed knife. Return to the freezer for at least 2–3 hours or overnight, or until solid.

10 To serve, remove the set pie from the tin. Gently peel off the lining paper and dust lightly with icing sugar and cocoa powder. Sprinkle with the chocolate curls. Allow to soften at room temperature for 10–15 minutes before cutting.

Note
If you don't want to use the whole of the pie at once, it can be cut into serving portions at the end of step 9.

Overleaf: Frozen Mississippi Mud Pie

Cassata

This Neapolitan speciality is traditionally served at Easter or other festivities, such as weddings. In its native country it is shaped in a special metal container called a *stampo da spumante*, which is dome-shaped with a lid, similar to our 'bombe' mould. We found it just as easy to layer up the ice cream in a pudding basin and the results were just as stunning. Cassata needs a lot of on-off attention, so start making it early in the day.

SERVES 8

For the ice cream
3 egg yolks
75 g (3 oz) caster sugar
300 ml (½ pint) milk
50 g (2 oz) plain chocolate
225 g (8 oz) ripe strawberries,
hulled and sliced
1.25 ml (¼ tsp) vanilla essence
150 ml (¼ pint) double cream

For the chantilly cream
15 g (½ oz) pistachio nuts
150 ml (¼ pint) double cream
1 egg white
50 g (2 oz) caster sugar
grated rind of 1 lemon

For the sauce
350 g (12 oz) ripe strawberries,
hulled
45 ml (3 level tbsp) icing sugar
15–30 ml (1–2 tbsp) Cointreau

1 To make the basic ice cream mixture, whisk the egg yolks and caster sugar together until pale and thick. Heat the milk until it almost reaches boiling point, and pour on to the egg mixture, whisking well. Strain back into the pan and cook for 10–12 minutes over a low heat, stirring all the time, until the custard thickens slightly. Do not boil. Strain into a bowl and cool.

2 Melt the chocolate with 15 ml (1 tbsp) milk (see page 12). Stir gently until smooth. Meanwhile, purée the 225 g (8 oz) strawberries in a blender or food processor, then push through a nylon sieve to extract most of the seeds. Add two thirds of the cool custard to the chocolate, stirring to blend. Stir the remaining custard and the vanilla essence into the strawberry purée.

3 Lightly whip the cream until it just begins to hold its shape. Stir two thirds into the cold chocolate mixture and the remainder into the strawberry purée. Pour into separate shallow freezer containers, cover and freeze by hand (see page 112).

4 Place a disc of non-stick baking parchment in the base of a 1.1 litre (2 pint) pudding basin. Place the empty basin in the freezer. Leave the chocolate ice cream at room temperature for about 20 minutes to soften slightly. Line the basin evenly with chocolate ice cream, using a metal spoon. Freeze for about 1½ hours or until firm.

5 Take the strawberry ice cream out of the freezer and leave at room temperature for 20–30 minutes to soften slightly. Again working with a spoon to make it more pliable (it will be firmer than the chocolate ice cream), use to make a second lining of ice cream in the basin. Cover and freeze until firm.

6 Pour boiling water over the pistachio nuts, leave to stand for 10 minutes, then skin and roughly chop. Whip the cream until it just holds its shape. Whisk the egg white until stiff but not dry. Whisk in the sugar until smooth, then fold in the cream with the nuts and grated lemon rind.

7 Spoon the chantilly cream into the centre of the ice cream layers and level off the top. Cover and freeze for 4–4½ hours or until firm.

8 Meanwhile, to prepare the sauce, slice the strawberries. Purée the strawberries with the icing sugar and Cointreau in a blender or food processor. Press the purée through a nylon sieve to remove the small seeds. Chill well before serving with the cassata.

9 To remove the cassata from the mould, place in the fridge for 10 minutes to soften slightly. Immerse the sides of the pudding basin in lukewarm water for about 15 seconds. Gently loosen the top edges of the ice cream, invert on to a serving plate and shake gently. Carefully lift off the mould and discard the paper disc. Return to the freezer to firm up the outside if necessary. Cut into wedges to serve.

Individual Coffee Bombes with Truffle Centres

These delicious bombes with a surprise centre will not fail to impress. Replace the Chocolate Flake Ice Cream with any of the others in this chapter, if preferred.

SERVES 6

1½ quantities Chocolate Flake Ice Cream (see page 114)

For the filling
25 g (1 oz) cake crumbs
25 g (1 oz) ground almonds
50 g (2 oz) plain chocolate
45 ml (3 tbsp) double cream
30 ml (2 tbsp) rum or brandy
chocolate leaves (see page 15) or
caraque (see page 13), to decorate

1 Set the freezer to fast-freeze. Put six 175 ml (6 fl oz) individual freezerproof pie or pudding moulds, or ramekin dishes, in the freezer to chill.

2 Leave the ice cream at room temperature for 20–30 minutes or until soft enough to spread.

3 Meanwhile, to make the truffle filling, mix the cake crumbs and almonds together in a bowl. Melt the chocolate with the cream (see page 12). Add the chocolate mixture to the crumb and almond mixture with the rum. Mix well.

4 Spread the softened ice cream around the base and sides of the moulds or dishes, leaving a cavity in the centre for the truffle mixture. Freeze for 1 hour or until firm.

5 Fill the centre of each mould with the truffle mixture and level the surface. Cover and freeze for 1 hour or until firm.

6 To serve, dip the moulds or dishes briefly in hot water, then unmould on to serving plates. Return to the freezer for 10 minutes to firm up. Decorate and serve.

FROZEN CHOCOLATE, RUM AND RAISIN CAKE

SERVES 12

For the filling
50 g (2 oz) raisins
60 ml (4 tbsp) dark rum
50 g (2 oz) caster sugar
3 egg yolks
175 g (6 oz) plain chocolate
300 ml (½ pint) double cream

For the biscuit crust
75 g (3 oz) butter or margarine, melted
225 g (8 oz) plain chocolate digestive biscuits, crushed

1 Put the raisins and rum in a small bowl and leave to soak for several hours or overnight.

2 To make the biscuit crust, mix the butter and biscuits together. Press into the base of a 20.5 cm (8 inch) spring-release cake tin. Chill for 30 minutes or overnight.

3 To make the filling, put the sugar and 75 ml (5 tbsp) water in a small saucepan and heat gently until the sugar has dissolved. Increase the heat and boil the mixture rapidly for 4 minutes to make a syrup.

4 Meanwhile, drain the raisins, reserving any excess rum. Lightly whisk the egg yolks with the reserved rum. Gradually pour the sugar syrup on to the egg yolks, whisking all the time.

5 Melt the chocolate (see page 12). Stir into the egg yolk mixture and leave to cool.

6 Whip the cream until stiff, then fold into the cold chocolate mixture. Fold in the raisins. Pour the mixture into the tin on top of the biscuit base.

7 Cover tightly with cling film and foil, then freeze for at least 3–4 hours or until firm. Remove from the freezer for 5 minutes before serving cut into wedges.

CHOCOLATE SORBET

This is delicious served with a little Kahlua or Tia Maria poured over.

SERVES 4

125 g (4 oz) granulated sugar
25 g (1 oz) cocoa powder
2.5 ml (½ level tsp) instant coffee powder
1 egg white

1 Put the sugar, cocoa powder and 300 ml (½ pint) water in a heavy-based saucepan. Heat gently until the sugar dissolves, then bring to the boil and boil rapidly for 2 minutes, without stirring. Remove from the heat, add the coffee powder and stir until dissolved. Leave to cool completely.

2 Pour the mixture into a shallow freezer container, cover and freeze for about 3 hours or until mushy.

3 Whisk the egg white until stiff. Turn the sorbet into a bowl and beat gently to break down the ice crystals. Fold in the egg white. Return to the freezer container, cover and freeze for 4 hours or until firm.

4 Transfer the sorbet to the refrigerator for about 10 minutes to soften slightly before serving.

CHAPTER SIX

CONFECTIONERY

● For a smooth, shiny, professional finish, there is no doubt that tempered couverture chocolate (see page 21) really does give the best result when making dipped chocolates. It is very viscous after tempering, making dipping easy. The chocolate sets to give a fine, crisp coating and it will not develop 'bloom' during storage. The taste of a thin coating of really good bittersweet chocolate is far superior to any of the alternatives and well worth the effort of tempering. It is extremely difficult to apply a thin, even coating of ordinary chocolate (by 'ordinary', we mean the kind bought for eating in sweet shops or supermarkets) because it is not fluid enough, so we do not recommend you use this for dipping chocolates.

● If you intend to make a lot of chocolate-coated confectionery, it is worth investing in a proper dipping fork or ring. This makes dipping easier, because a dipping fork has a long, straight handle and long, thin tines. After dipping, the fork may be used to give a professional decoration to the chocolate (see right).

● A wide, fairly shallow bowl is best for dipping; a very deep bowl makes the action of lifting out the chocolates awkward.

● To achieve the perfect coating, a certain amount of practice and technique is required. Fully immerse the chosen chocolate centre in the melted chocolate, turn it around so that it is fully coated on all sides, then lift it up out of the chocolate by placing the fork tines or ring underneath it. Do not spear it. Lightly tap the neck of the fork on the edge of the bowl so that any excess chocolate runs back into the bowl.

Repeat this action a couple of times until the chocolate stops dripping, then draw the fork back across the bowl rim so that any excess chocolate that has collected on the base of the chocolate is wiped off. Carefully flip the chocolate over on to a piece of waxed paper so that what was the top becomes the underside. (This gives a neater result than if you try to slide the chocolate off the fork – and it is easier than it sounds.) Decorate as desired (see below) before the chocolate sets. If your dipping has been successful, the finished chocolate will be without a pool, or 'foot' (as it is known in the trade), of chocolate at the base. Leave to set at room temperature. If you've used tempered chocolate, it will set very quickly.

● To give a professional finish, decorate the tops of the sweets by touching them with the tines of a dipping fork or with a dipping ring. Do this immediately the chocolate has been dipped. Touch the surface with the fork or ring, then gently lift it up slightly (so that it is still in contact with the chocolate coating but not pressing on the centre) and glide it across the surface. Your technique will improve with practice; once you've done this a few times, it becomes easy and very satisfying.

● Resist touching the chocolates while they are setting, or the smooth glossy surface will be ruined. The chocolate coating will be shinier if allowed to cool at room temperature (and if tempered chocolate or a very good quality chocolate has been used). In very hot weather, it may be necessary to refrigerate the chocolate to help it to set.

FRESH CREAM TRUFFLES

Coat just a few truffles at a time and put them into the refrigerator immediately. If you try to coat the whole batch, the first ones may start to melt.

MAKES ABOUT 45

150 ml (¼ pint) double cream
1 vanilla pod
1 egg yolk
25 g (1 oz) caster sugar
150 g (5 oz) plain chocolate, broken into pieces
25 g (1 oz) unsalted butter, softened

For the decoration
150 g (5 oz) couverture chocolate or one of the alternatives (see page 22)
75 g (3 oz) good quality white chocolate
50 g (2 oz) white chocolate flavour cake covering

1 Place the double cream and vanilla pod in a small saucepan. Bring to the boil, cover and remove from the heat. Leave the mixture to infuse for 20 minutes. Remove the vanilla pod.

2 Whisk the egg yolk with the sugar until very pale and thick. Whisk into the cream and return to the heat. Heat gently, without boiling, for 2–3 minutes or until it is beginning to thicken, stirring all the time. Remove from the heat.

3 Add the plain chocolate and stir until completely melted. Refrigerate the mixture for about 1 hour or until firm.

4 Using an electric whisk, whisk the softened butter into the chocolate and cream mixture.

5 Spoon the mixture into a piping bag fitted with a 1 cm (½ inch) plain nozzle and pipe 2.5 cm (1 inch) lengths on to a flat plate or baking sheet. Freeze for about 1 hour or until the cream has set completely.

6 To decorate, temper the couverture chocolate (see page 21) or melt one of the alternatives (see page 12). Melt the white chocolate with the white chocolate flavour cake covering.

7 Coat half of the truffles in the plain chocolate and half in the white chocolate (see page 124 for detailed instructions on dipping). Pipe or drizzle white chocolate over the plain chocolate-covered truffles and plain chocolate over the white chocolate-covered truffles. Refrigerate until set. Store in the refrigerator until required.

Overleaf: Fresh Cream Truffles

QUICK AND EASY TRUFFLES

Truffles based on sponge cake crumbs are easier to handle than the classic chocolate and cream mixture (see Fresh Cream Truffles, page 125).

MAKES ABOUT 24

125 g (4 oz) plain chocolate
50 g (2 oz) unsalted butter
125 g (4 oz) trifle sponge cakes,
crumbled
50 g (2 oz) icing sugar
25 ml (1½ tbsp) dark rum, brandy
or liqueur of your choice
50 g (2 oz) cocoa powder, icing
sugar or chocolate vermicelli

1 Melt the chocolate with the butter (see page 12). Stir in the cake crumbs, icing sugar and spirit or liqueur of your choice. Cover and refrigerate for about 30 minutes or until the mixture is firm enough to handle.
2 Lightly dust your fingers with icing sugar and roll the truffle mixture into 24 small balls, then roll each one in the cocoa powder, icing sugar or chocolate vermicelli to coat completely.
3 Arrange the truffles in petit four cases, then chill in the refrigerator until required. Remove from the refrigerator about 30 minutes before serving.

CHOCOLATE NUT TRUFFLES

Crumbs from a plain Victoria sponge cake are best for this recipe.

MAKES ABOUT 30

125 g (4 oz) shelled hazelnuts
125 g (4 oz) plain chocolate
75 g (3 oz) butter, diced
150 g (5 oz) cake crumbs
30 ml (2 level tbsp) icing sugar
about 30 ml (2 tbsp) rum or brandy
cocoa powder for coating

1 Toast the nuts under the grill until brown. Tip into a clean tea-towel and rub off the skins. When cold, grind in a mill or food processor.
2 Melt the chocolate (see page 12). Cool slightly, then stir in the butter until evenly blended. Add the nuts with the cake crumbs, icing sugar and rum or brandy to taste.
3 Chill the mixture in the refrigerator until firm, then roll into small balls and place on a baking sheet lined with waxed paper.
4 Refrigerate, covered, until firm, then coat lightly in cocoa powder and return to the refrigerator until required. These truffles soften quickly at room temperature.

BITTER ORANGE CHOCOLATES

MAKES ABOUT 24

*150 g (5 oz) couverture chocolate or
one of the alternatives (see page 22)
finely grated rind and juice of
1 orange
5 ml (1 level tsp) granulated sugar
225 g (8 oz) white chocolate
75 ml (3 fl oz) double cream
25 g (1 oz) unsalted butter
chopped almonds and icing sugar,
to decorate (optional)*

1 Temper the couverture chocolate (see page 21) or melt one of the alternatives (see page 12). Brush half the chocolate over the insides of 24 paper petit four cases. Chill until firm. Use the remaining melted chocolate to brush on a second coat. Chill until firm.
2 Strain 45 ml (3 tbsp) orange juice into a saucepan, add the sugar and heat gently until the sugar has dissolved. Bring to the boil and boil rapidly for 3–4 minutes to reduce to 30 ml (2 tbsp). Cool.
3 Melt the white chocolate with the cream (see page 12). Remove from the heat and whisk in the orange syrup and grated orange rind. Gradually beat in the butter. Cool until the mixture is the consistency of whipped cream, then pipe or spoon into the cases. Sprinkle with the almonds and dust with icing sugar, if using. Cover loosely and store in the refrigerator.

Variation

Liqueur Chocolates Replace the orange syrup with 30 ml (2 tbsp) liqueur, such as Cointreau or Drambuie.

CINNAMON MERINGUE HEARTS

Small meringues are ideal as petits fours. Alternatively, pipe larger shapes about 5 cm (2 inches) long and serve as a dessert with a little single cream to accompany.

MAKES ABOUT 70

*2 egg whites
125 g (4 oz) caster sugar
2.5 ml (½ level tsp) ground
cinnamon, sifted
15 ml (1 level tbsp) cocoa powder,
sifted*

For the filling and decoration
*150 ml (¼ pint) double cream
125 g (4 oz) plain chocolate
cocoa powder and icing sugar*

1 Line two baking sheets with non-stick baking parchment.
2 Whisk the egg whites until stiff but not dry. Whisk in half the sugar until the mixture is stiff and shiny. Carefully fold in the remaining sugar with the cinnamon and cocoa powder.
3 Spoon the meringue into a piping bag fitted with a small, plain 0.5 cm (¼ inch) nozzle and pipe small heart shapes about 2.5 cm (1 inch) long on to the lined baking sheets.
4 Bake in the oven at 140°C (275°F) mark 1 for about 1 hour or until completely dried out. Remove with a palette knife and transfer to a wire rack to cool. Store in an airtight container if not using immediately.
5 To make the filling, put the cream in a saucepan and bring to the boil. Meanwhile, chop the chocolate. Pour the cream over the chocolate, leave for 5 minutes, then whisk until thoroughly mixed. Chill until firm.
6 About 1 hour before serving, sandwich the meringues together with the filling.
7 Dust with cocoa powder and icing sugar. Refrigerate for up to 2 hours.

SOLID CHOCOLATE EGGS

Ensure that the egg shells are thoroughly washed and dried before adding the chocolate.

MAKES 4

4 eggs
450 g (1 lb) couverture chocolate,
tempered (see page 21), or plain,
milk or white chocolate

For the decoration
crystallised violets
crystallised rose petals
melted chocolate

1 If you have never blown an egg before, now is the time to try. With a needle, pierce a tiny hole in each end of one of the eggs and blow out the contents. Enlarge the hole in one end to take a small piping nozzle and wash out the shell with cold water. Leave to dry thoroughly while you blow the rest of the eggs. (The warmth of a radiator will help with this.) When they are dry, put a piece of sticky tape over the small hole in each egg so that it cannot leak.

2 Melt the chocolate (see page 12), if necessary. (If using tempered couverture chocolate, it will already be melted.)

3 Spoon the melted chocolate into a nylon piping bag fitted with a small nozzle and pipe into the egg shells through the large holes. Swirl it round from time to time to remove any air bubbles. Leave the eggs overnight to set.

4 Carefully crack the eggs and peel off the shells. Decorate the solid chocolate eggs with crystallised violets, rose petals and narrow ribbons, sticking them on with melted chocolate. Alternatively, wrap each egg tightly in coloured foil. Place them in egg cups or arrange in a basket.

Variation
Marbled Eggs To make solid marbled Easter eggs, fill plastic egg moulds with alternate spoonfuls of melted plain and white chocolate. Tap on the work surface to remove any air bubbles, then leave to set. Unmould the egg halves and stick together with a little melted chocolate.

CHOCOLATE EASTER EGG

Add liqueur to the truffles sparingly, or they'll turn out too soft. You may need to firm up the mixture in the refrigerator between shapings, anyway. The truffle recipe will fill two eggs; don't be tempted to use half quantity, or it will be difficult to work.

MAKES ONE 15 CM (6 INCH) EGG

275–325 g (10–11½ oz) couverture chocolate, tempered (see page 21), or plain, milk or white chocolate

For the truffles
225 g (8 oz) plain or milk chocolate
75 ml (3 fl oz) double cream
a few drops of brandy, rum, orange-flavoured liqueur, coffee essence or vanilla essence, to taste
chopped nuts, desiccated coconut, chocolate vermicelli or grated chocolate for coating

To assemble
melted chocolate
ribbons
flowers (optional)

1 Using cotton wool, polish the insides of two 15 cm (6 inch) plastic Easter egg moulds. Place on a tray lined with non-stick baking parchment.
2 Melt the chocolate (see page 12), if necessary. (If using tempered chocolate it will already be melted.) Remove from the heat and leave to cool slightly.
3 Using a large spoon, pour enough melted chocolate into each mould in turn to coat the sides. Tilt the moulds to coat completely.
4 Pour the excess chocolate back into the bowl. Invert the moulds on to the non-stick baking parchment and refrigerate briefly until set. Apply a second coat of chocolate

and refrigerate again. Repeat once more, then return to the refrigerator and leave for 1 hour or until set. (If using tempered chocolate, aim to do these three coats before the chocolate sets in the bowl, or it will have to be re-tempered. If not using tempered chocolate, it can be re-melted if necessary.) The eggs will crack if removed from the refrigerator too soon.
5 To turn out the chocolate egg halves, trim any excess chocolate from the outer edge of the moulds. Carefully pull each mould away from the chocolate around the edge to let air get in between the chocolate and the mould. Press firmly and the chocolate should slip out. Cover loosely and refrigerate.
6 To make the truffles, grate the chocolate into a small saucepan and add the cream. Heat gently until the chocolate has melted. Stir well and remove from the heat. Cool to room temperature.
7 The mixture should have thickened considerably. Beat in the desired flavouring, then, preferably using an electric whisk or mixer, beat for about 5 minutes or until the mixture is light and stands in peaks. Cover and refrigerate until quite firm.
8 Sprinkle a tray with your desired coating. Place teaspoonfuls of truffle mixture on a cool work surface. Dust your hands with cocoa powder or icing sugar and quickly roll the mixture into balls. Roll the truffles in the coating and place on a baking sheet lined with non-stick baking parchment. Cover and refrigerate. The truffles will keep for 4 days in the refrigerator.
9 To assemble the Easter egg, put the truffles in paper sweet cases or cellophane wrapping. Fill one half of the Easter egg with some of the truffles. Spread a little melted chocolate over the rims of the egg and, holding the remaining half in non-stick baking parchment, press it on to the melted chocolate to complete the egg. Refrigerate to set. Tie ribbons around the middle and decorate with flowers, if liked.

CHOCOLATE-COATED PECANS

Make sure the nut mixture is well chilled before coating and the chocolate will set quickly.

MAKES ABOUT 35

about 200 g (7 oz) pecan nuts
25 g (1 oz) icing sugar
50 g (2 oz) plain or milk chocolate, chopped
15 g (½ oz) unsalted butter
175 g (6 oz) couverture chocolate or one of the alternatives (see page 22)

1 Put 50 g (2 oz) of the nuts, the icing sugar, the chopped chocolate and the butter in a food processor. Process until smooth.
2 Roll the mixture into small walnut-sized balls. Sandwich between two pecan halves and chill until firm.
3 Temper the couverture chocolate (see page 21) or melt one of the alternatives (see page 12). Dip the nuts into the chocolate to coat completely (see page 124 for detailed instructions on dipping). Leave to set on waxed paper. Store in a single layer in an airtight container.

CHOCOLATE WALNUT CREAMS

The soft, smooth, nutty paste provides a delightful contrast in texture to the walnut halves. The distinctive shape of the walnut under the chocolate means that no final decoration is needed.

MAKES ABOUT 50

275 g (10 oz) walnut halves
125 g (4 oz) caster sugar
15 ml (1 tbsp) orange juice
200 g (7 oz) couverture chocolate or one of the alternatives (see page 22)

1 Grind 125 g (4 oz) of the walnuts in a mill or food processor. Mix the ground nuts and sugar in a bowl, then add the orange juice and mix together to form a light paste. Knead the paste with your fingers until firm.
2 Roll out the walnut paste to about 0.5 cm (¼ inch) thick on a board lightly dusted with icing sugar. Cut into circles, using a 2.5 cm (1 inch) plain round cutter. Press a walnut half firmly into each circle of paste.
3 Temper the chocolate (see page 21) or melt one of the alternatives (see page 12).
4 Dip the walnut rounds one at a time into the chocolate to give them a generous coating (see page 124 for detailed instructions on dipping). Place on waxed paper to dry.

FILLED MOULDED CHOCOLATES

These are made in special moulds which are available from good cookshops. It is difficult to give exact quantities since the moulds vary, but the basic method is always the same.

Chocolate moulds come in a variety of shapes and sizes. Some come as plastic or rubber sheets of moulds, while individual metal or plastic shapes are available. Depending on their size, they may be coated with a thin layer of chocolate and filled with ganache (see page 152), marzipan or fondant; see below for the method. Alternatively, some have two halves (like an Easter egg mould) and may be used to make hollow shapes. Larger moulds used to make hollow chocolate shapes will require at least two coats of chocolate for strength. Tempered couverture chocolate (see page 21) is easiest to handle and gives a professional, glossy finish that will last and not bloom. Ordinary melted chocolate can be used with satisfactory results for large moulds, such as Easter eggs (see page 132). For alternatives to tempered couverture, see page 22.

It is quicker and easier to make filled chocolates in moulds than to make individually dipped chocolates. Before you start, ensure that the moulds are perfectly clean and dry, then polish them to a real shine with cotton wool. (The more you polish, the shinier the chocolate will be.) Use a small ladle or jug to fill the indentations with tempered couverture chocolate or one of the alternatives (see page 22). Tap the mould sharply on the work surface to remove any air bubbles. Leave for a few minutes to settle, then invert over the bowl of melted chocolate and let most of it run out of the moulds, leaving a thin coating behind. Run a clean palette knife across the top to scrape off any excess, then leave to set.

Once set, add the filling of your choice, filling the moulds almost to the top. If using ganache, it's easiest to pipe it in with a piping bag. If using fondant or marzipan, roll it into small balls and press gently into the chocolate-lined indentations. Pour over more chocolate to seal in the filling. Tap the mould on the work surface to remove any air bubbles and scrape off excess chocolate with a palette knife. Leave to set, then unmould.

WHITE CHOCOLATE COLETTES

MAKES ABOUT 16

50 g (2 oz) good quality white chocolate
50 g (2 oz) white chocolate flavour cake covering

For the filling and decoration
50 g (2 oz) good quality white chocolate
25 g (1 oz) butter
10 ml (2 tsp) brandy
60 ml (4 tbsp) double cream
crystallised violets

1 Arrange 16 double petit four cases on a baking sheet. Melt the chocolate and chocolate flavour cake covering together (see page 12). Spoon a little into each paper case and use a brush to spread it to coat the inside of each case completely. Chill until set. Re-melt the chocolate and repeat the process to make a thick chocolate shell.
2 To make the filling, melt the chocolate with the butter and brandy. Remove from the heat and leave for about 10 minutes or until cool but not set.
3 Meanwhile, carefully peel away the paper from the chocolate cases. Whisk the cream into the cooled chocolate mixture and leave until thick enough to pipe. Spoon into a piping bag fitted with a small star nozzle and pipe into the chocolate cases. Decorate with crystallised violets. Chill the colettes in the refrigerator for at least 1 hour before serving.

CHEATS' CHOCOLATE AND NUT FUDGE

No fiddling with thermometers required for this melt-in-the-mouth fudge that only takes a few minutes to prepare. If you own a microwave, you can make it even quicker by melting the chocolate and butter with the milk on HIGH for 2–3 minutes. If using hazelnuts or macadamia nuts, the finished result will be improved if you toast the nuts before adding them to the fudge.

MAKES ABOUT 450 G (1 LB)

125 g (4 oz) butter, diced
75 g (3 oz) plain chocolate, chopped
60 ml (4 tbsp) milk or single cream
60 ml (4 level tbsp) cocoa powder
400 g (14 oz) icing sugar
125 g (4 oz) Brazil nuts, hazelnuts or macadamia nuts, roughly chopped

1 Grease a shallow 18 cm (7 inch) square tin and line with greaseproof paper.
2 Put the butter, chocolate and milk or cream in a large heatproof bowl. Stand the bowl over a saucepan of simmering water and stir until the chocolate has melted.
3 Meanwhile, sift the cocoa powder with the icing sugar. As soon as the chocolate has melted, tip the sugar mixture into the bowl and beat together until smooth. Beat in three quarters of the nuts. Pour into the prepared tin, then tap vigorously on the work surface to level the surface of the fudge. Sprinkle the remaining nuts on top and press down lightly. Chill in the refrigerator until set, then cut into small squares. This fudge has a soft set, so it is best kept in the refrigerator.

CHOCOLATE FUDGE

MAKES ABOUT 800 G (1¾ LB)

450 g (1 lb) granulated sugar
150 ml (¼ pint) milk
150 g (5 oz) butter
150 g (5 oz) plain chocolate, broken
into pieces
50 g (2 oz) honey

1 Lightly oil an 18 cm (7 inch) shallow square tin.
2 Heat all the ingredients gently in a large heavy-based saucepan, stirring until the sugar has dissolved.
3 Bring to the boil without stirring, then continue boiling until a temperature of 115°C (240°F) is reached, stirring occasionally to prevent sticking. (Check the temperature on a sugar thermometer.)
4 Remove the pan from the heat and stand it on a cool surface for 5 minutes, then beat the mixture until thick, creamy and beginning to 'grain'.
5 Pour into the prepared tin, mark into squares when almost set and cut when cold.

CHOCOLATE ALMOND CRUNCH

The crunchy praline chocolate centres make a good contrast to the smooth chocolate coating. Crystallised violets make pretty decorations, but if you prefer to keep to nuts, top each chocolate with a flake of toasted almond.

MAKES ABOUT 25 PIECES

75 g (3 oz) whole unblanched
almonds
75 g (3 oz) caster sugar
200 g (7 oz) plain chocolate
125 g (4 oz) good quality white
chocolate
75 g (3 oz) white chocolate flavour
cake covering
crystallised violets or toasted flaked
almonds, to decorate

1 Oil a baking sheet. Put the almonds and sugar in a small, heavy-based saucepan and heat very gently until the sugar has dissolved, stirring to prevent the sugar sticking to the pan. Continue to heat until the sugar caramelises to a light golden colour and the nuts are lightly toasted.
2 Pour the mixture on to the prepared baking sheet and leave to set. When completely hard, finely crush the praline with a rolling pin or grind in a mill or food processor.
3 Melt the plain chocolate (see page 12). Mix in the praline to make a stiff paste and turn it into an 18 cm (7 inch) square tin. Leave to set.
4 Cut the chocolate praline into squares. Melt the white chocolate and white chocolate flavour cake covering (see page 12). Dip the chocolate praline, one piece at a time, into the chocolate to give a generous coating (see page 124 for detailed instructions on dipping). Before the coating dries, decorate each square with a piece of crystallised violet. Leave to set on waxed paper.

HONEY AND CHOCOLATE FUDGE

The honey used in this recipe not only gives the fudge flavour, but stops it crystallising as well, making it deliciously soft and creamy textured.

MAKES ABOUT 700 G (I½ LB)

450 g (1 lb) caster sugar
45 ml (3 tbsp) clear honey
450 ml (¾ pint) sweetened
condensed milk
125 g (4 oz) butter
125 g (4 oz) plain chocolate,
chopped
a few drops of vanilla essence

1 Oil an 18 cm (7 inch) square tin. Put the sugar, honey, condensed milk and butter in a large, heavy-based saucepan and heat gently until the butter has melted and the sugar has completely dissolved, stirring continuously. Bring to the boil and boil to 115°C (240°F), stirring occasionally. (Check the temperature on a sugar thermometer.)
2 Remove the pan from the heat and beat in the chocolate and vanilla essence. Cool a little, then beat until the mixture is thick enough to leave a trail when the whisk is lifted.
3 Pour the fudge into the prepared tin and leave to cool. Mark into squares as it begins to set. When completely cold and set, turn the fudge out and cut into the marked squares.

RUM AND RAISIN CUPS

There is a superb surprise filling of sponge and raisins soaked in rum when you bite into these chocolates. They make a perfect Christmas gift.

MAKES ABOUT 40

150 g (5 oz) couverture chocolate
150 g (5 oz) plain chocolate flavour
cake covering
125 g (4 oz) stale sponge cake
65 g (2½ oz) raisins
120 ml (8 tbsp) rum

1 Melt together the couverture and chocolate flavour cake covering (see page 12). Using foil sweet cases or double paper petit four cases as moulds, spoon a little chocolate into each case and use a small brush to coat the inside of each case completely. Leave to dry upside-down on non-stick baking parchment. Repeat, making about 40 chocolate cups. Apply a second coat of chocolate if the first one looks thin. Leave to set.
2 Crumble the sponge and mix in the raisins. Cover with rum and leave to soak for about 30 minutes or until all the rum is soaked up.
3 Spoon a little of the soaked cake and raisin mixture into the chocolate cups. Remelt the chocolate. Flood the tops of the cups, covering the filling completely to the edges. Leave to set.
4 When the tops are thoroughly dry, peel off the cases and place the chocolate cups in fresh cases.

CHAPTER SEVEN

BISCUITS
AND
COOKIES

CHOCOLATE NUT SNAPS

(Photograph on page 115)
If you haven't got time to make a paper icing bag, drizzle the chocolate decoration on to the biscuits from a teaspoon.

MAKES ABOUT 24

1 egg, separated
125 g (4 oz) caster sugar
75 g (3 oz) plain chocolate, finely chopped
125 g (4 oz) hazelnuts, toasted, skinned and finely chopped
50 g (2 oz) plain flour
50 g (2 oz) ground almonds

For the decoration
50 g (2 oz) plain or white chocolate icing sugar for dusting

1 Grease two baking sheets. Whisk the egg white until stiff, then stir in the remaining ingredients (including the egg yolk). Work the mixture with your fingers until it forms a ball.
2 Turn the dough out on to a lightly floured surface, knead lightly and roll out until it is about 0.5 cm (¼ inch) thick. Using a 5 cm (2 inch) cutter, cut out about 24 biscuits, re-kneading and re-rolling the trimmings as necessary. Arrange the biscuits on the prepared baking sheets.
3 Bake in the oven at 190°C (375°F) mark 5 for 12–15 minutes or until crisp. Immediately ease the cooked biscuits off the baking sheets, put them on a wire rack and leave to cool.
4 To decorate the biscuits, melt the chocolate (see page 12) and leave to cool slightly. Lightly dust the biscuits with icing sugar. Make a greaseproof paper piping bag and spoon in the melted chocolate. Snip off the tip of the bag and pipe lines of chocolate across the biscuits. Leave to set.

CHOCOLATE AND GINGER THINS

MAKES ABOUT 20

125 g (4 oz) butter or margarine
175 g (6 oz) plain flour
50 g (2 oz) caster sugar
25 g (1 oz) plain chocolate, finely chopped
25 g (1 oz) stem ginger, finely chopped

For the icing
125 g (4 oz) icing sugar
10 ml (2 level tsp) cocoa powder
a knob of butter

1 Rub the butter into the flour and stir in the sugar, chocolate and ginger. Knead together with your fingers until the mixture sticks together.
2 Turn the dough on to a lightly floured surface and roll it out thinly. Using a 6.5 cm (2½ inch) fluted cutter, cut out about 20 biscuits, re-kneading and re-rolling the trimmings as necessary. Arrange on greased baking sheets and bake in the oven at 190°C (375°F) mark 5 for 12–15 minutes or until just golden brown. Transfer to a wire rack and leave to cool.
3 To make the icing, sift together the icing sugar and cocoa powder into a bowl. Add the butter and 30 ml (2 tbsp) hot water and blend until smooth. Dip half of each biscuit in the icing, then leave to set on a wire rack.

ORANGE AND CHOCOLATE LOGS

These little logs are delicious plain or dipped in chocolate.

MAKES ABOUT 60

250 g (9 oz) butter or margarine,
softened
50 g (2 oz) icing sugar
finely grated rind and juice of
1 orange
225 g (8 oz) plain flour
75 g (3 oz) cornflour
75 g (3 oz) plain chocolate

1 Cream the butter and sugar together until pale and fluffy. Beat in the orange rind and 30 ml (2 tbsp) strained orange juice.
2 Sift in the flours and mix until thoroughly smooth. Spoon the mixture into a piping bag fitted with a 1 cm (½ inch) star nozzle.
3 Pipe the mixture on to greased baking sheets, making about 60 small logs 4–5 cm (1½–2 inches) long.
4 Bake at 180°C (350°F) mark 4 for about 15 minutes or until sandy brown and just firm to the touch. Transfer to a wire rack and leave to cool.
5 Melt the chocolate (see page 12) and leave to cool slightly. Dip in each log to half-coat in chocolate, then allow to dry on a wire rack.

FLORENTINES

To make more elaborate florentines, for serving as petits fours, make them slightly smaller than here. Coat half with plain and half with milk chocolate, then pipe with contrasting lines of chocolate to decorate.

MAKES ABOUT 30

100 g (3½ oz) butter
125 g (4 oz) caster sugar
125 g (4 oz) flaked almonds,
roughly chopped
25 g (1 oz) sultanas
5 glacé cherries, chopped
25 g (1 oz) chopped mixed peel
15 ml (1 tbsp) single cream or milk
275 g (10 oz) plain chocolate

1 Line four baking sheets with non-stick baking parchment. Melt the butter in a saucepan over a low heat, add the sugar and boil the mixture for 1 minute.
2 Remove the pan from the heat and add all the remaining ingredients, except the chocolate, stirring well to mix.
3 Drop the mixture in small heaps on to the prepared baking sheets, allowing space between each for the mixture to spread.
4 Bake in the oven at 180°C (350°F) mark 4 for 10–15 minutes or until golden brown.
5 Remove from the oven and press around the edges of the biscuits with the blade of a knife to neaten the shape. Leave on the baking sheets for 5 minutes or until beginning to firm, then cool on a wire rack.
6 When the biscuits are cool, melt the chocolate (see page 12) and leave it to cool for about 10–15 minutes or until it coats the back of a spoon and is just beginning to set.
7 Spread the chocolate over the backs of the biscuits. Mark wavy lines in the chocolate with a fork and leave to set.

Overleaf: Florentines

CHOCOLATE AND HONEY FUDGE FINGERS

Divide this into small fingers as it's quite rich to eat. It's easy to make double the quantity and then keep a supply in the refrigerator; it will soon disappear!

MAKES ABOUT 12

225 g (8 oz) digestive wheatmeal or
any plain biscuits
75 g (3 oz) raisins
50 g (2 oz) plain chocolate
30 ml (2 tbsp) honey
75 g (3 oz) butter or margarine

1 Oil an 18 cm (7 inch) square tin and line the base with greaseproof paper.
2 Roughly crumble the biscuits and add the raisins. Melt the chocolate, honey and butter together in a small saucepan and stir into the biscuit crumbs.
3 Mix thoroughly and press firmly into the prepared tin.
4 Freeze for 10 minutes or chill until firm, then cut into fingers. Store in the refrigerator until required.

CHOCOLATE CHIP AND MACADAMIA COOKIES

For petit-four-sized cookies, roll the mixture into tiny balls, flatten and bake for about 7 minutes.

MAKES ABOUT 50

75 g (3 oz) butter or margarine,
softened
75 g (3 oz) granulated sugar
75 g (3 oz) light brown soft sugar
5 ml (1 tsp) vanilla essence
1 egg, beaten
175 g (6 oz) self-raising flour
a pinch of salt
125 g (4 oz) chocolate drops
75 g (3 oz) macadamia nuts,
roughly chopped

1 Cream the butter until very soft. Gradually beat in the sugars and vanilla essence until evenly blended. Add the beaten egg and mix well.
2 Sift the flour and salt into the bowl. Fold carefully into the creamed butter and sugar mixture.
3 Add the chocolate drops and 50 g (2 oz) of the macadamia nuts. Stir together to mix thoroughly.
4 Roll the mixture into balls about the size of marbles. Place on greased baking sheets, leaving space for spreading, and flatten lightly with a wet fork. Sprinkle the remaining chopped macadamia nuts on top of the biscuits, pressing them down lightly.
5 Bake at 180°C (350°F) mark 4 for about 10 minutes or until pale golden in colour. Leave to cool slightly on wire racks. These are best eaten warm.

ALMOND CHOCOLATE BISCUITS

MAKES ABOUT 48

200 g (7 oz) self-raising flour
150 g (5 oz) caster sugar
1.25 ml (¼ level tsp) freshly grated
nutmeg
150 g (5 oz) butter or margarine
125 g (4 oz) ground almonds
50 g (2 oz) plain, milk or white
chocolate, coarsely grated
1 egg, beaten
1.25 ml (¼ tsp) almond essence

1 Grease two or three baking sheets.
2 Put the flour, sugar and nutmeg in a bowl. Rub the butter into the flour mixture until it resembles fine crumbs. Stir in the almonds and 25 g (1 oz) chocolate. Bind together with the egg and almond essence, then knead until smooth.
3 On a lightly floured surface, divide the mixture into two and roll each part into a 30.5 cm (12 inch) long, thin sausage shape. Wrap in greaseproof paper or non-stick baking parchment.
4 Chill in the refrigerator for about 30 minutes or until firm. Cut the rolls into slices about 1 cm (½ inch) thick and place well apart on the baking sheets. Flatten them lightly with the back of your hand. Bake in rotation in the oven at 190°C (375°F) mark 5 for 15–20 minutes.
5 Let the biscuits cool until just warm, then sprinkle the remaining chocolate over. Transfer to a wire rack and leave to cool completely.

CHOCOLATE OATIES

MAKES ABOUT 40

175 g (6 oz) butter or margarine,
softened
200 g (7 oz) brown sugar
50 g (2 oz) plain chocolate
a large pinch of salt
2.5 ml (½ level tsp) baking powder
175 g (6 oz) plain flour
225 g (8 oz) rolled oats
30 ml (2 tbsp) milk
2.5 ml (½ tsp) vanilla essence

1 Cream the butter and sugar together until pale and fluffy. Meanwhile, melt the chocolate (see page 12) and leave to cool slightly.
2 Sift the salt, baking powder and flour into the creamed mixture and add half of the oats and all the remaining ingredients (including the chocolate). Mix well and shape the mixture into walnut-sized balls. Roll the balls in the remaining oats until coated on all sides.
3 Spread out the balls on lightly greased baking sheets and bake in the oven at 180°C (350°F) mark 4 for 25–30 minutes. Transfer to a wire rack and leave to cool.

MILLIONAIRES' SHORTBREAD

A wicked mixture of shortbread and caramel with a stunning marbled chocolate top. After sampling this, plain shortbread will never seem the same again!

MAKES ABOUT 12 SMALL SQUARES

75 g (3 oz) plain flour
25 g (1 oz) caster sugar
50 g (2 oz) butter

For the caramel and topping
50 g (2 oz) butter or margarine
50 g (2 oz) light brown soft sugar
397 g (14 oz) can condensed milk
75 g (3 oz) plain chocolate
75 g (3 oz) milk chocolate
75 g (3 oz) white chocolate

1 To make the shortbread, mix the flour and sugar together in a bowl. Rub in the butter until the mixture resembles fine breadcrumbs. Knead together until the mixture forms a ball, then press into the base of an 18 cm (7 inch) square tin.

2 Bake in the oven at 180°C (350°F) mark 4 for about 20 minutes or until firm to the touch and very lightly browned. Cool in the tin.

3 To make the caramel, put the butter, sugar and condensed milk in a saucepan and heat gently until the sugar has dissolved. Bring to the boil, stirring all the time, then reduce the heat and simmer very gently for about 5 minutes or until the mixture has thickened and is a creamy fudge colour. Pour over the shortbread and leave to cool.

4 When the caramel layer has cooled and set, melt the three different types of chocolate in separate bowls (see page 12). Place teaspoonfuls of the chocolate over the caramel, alternating the three types. Tap the tin on the work surface so that the different chocolates merge with each other, then use a skewer to create a marbled pattern. Chill until set, then cut into very small squares (it is very rich).

CHOCOLATE VIENNESE FINGERS

MAKES ABOUT 18

125 g (4 oz) butter or margarine,
softened
25 g (1 oz) icing sugar
25 g (1 oz) plain chocolate
125 g (4 oz) plain flour
1.25 ml (¼ level tsp) baking powder
15 ml (1 level tbsp) drinking
chocolate powder
a few drops of vanilla essence
50 g (2 oz) plain, milk or white
chocolate, to decorate

1 Grease two baking sheets. Put the butter in a bowl and beat until pale and soft, then beat in the icing sugar.

2 Melt the chocolate (see page 12) and leave to cool for 10 minutes. When the chocolate is cool, but not thick, beat it into the creamed mixture.

3 Sift in the flour, baking powder and drinking chocolate. Beat well, adding a few drops of vanilla essence.

4 Spoon into a piping bag fitted with a medium star nozzle and pipe finger shapes about 7.5 cm (3 inches) long on to the prepared baking sheets, allowing space between each for the mixture to spread. Bake at 190°C (375°F) mark 5 for 15–20 minutes or until crisp and pale golden. Transfer to a wire rack and leave to cool for 30 minutes.

5 When the biscuits are cold, melt the chocolate for the decoration and dip both ends of the fingers into it. Leave on a wire rack until set.

Variation

Plain Viennese Fingers Omit the drinking chocolate from the recipe above and add an extra 15 ml (1 level tbsp) plain flour.

TUILES

These biscuits have to be curled up the moment they come out of the oven so don't try to cook too many at once. If they're allowed to cool down, they'll refuse to roll. They don't contain any chocolate but make a delicious accompaniment to chocolate desserts, such as the Caramel Mousse on page 102.

MAKES ABOUT 24

2 egg whites
65 g (2½ oz) icing sugar, sifted
65 g (2½ oz) plain flour
65 g (2½ oz) butter, melted and
cooled
icing sugar for dusting

1 Beat together the egg whites, icing sugar and flour, then mix in the butter.

2 Spoon two small spoonfuls of mixture (about 7.5 ml/1½ level tsp each) on a baking sheet lined with non-stick baking parchment. Smooth into thin oblongs measuring about 4×20.5 cm (1½×8 inches).

3 Bake in the oven at 220°C (425°F) mark 7 for 3–4 minutes or until golden brown. *Immediately* remove from the paper using a palette knife and loosely roll each one around a wooden spoon handle. Once set, carefully remove from the spoon handle, place on a wire rack and leave to cool completely.

4 Repeat until all the mixture is used up, making about 24 tuiles. Once cold, place the tuiles in a well sealed rigid container with non-stick baking parchment between the layers. Store for up to a week.

5 Dust the tuiles with icing sugar to serve.

CHOCOLATE NUT BARS

MAKES ABOUT 16

125 g (4 oz) butter or margarine,
softened
50 g (2 oz) caster sugar
50 g (2 oz) dark brown soft sugar
1.25 ml (¼ level tsp) salt
5 ml (1 tsp) vanilla essence
125 g (4 oz) self-raising flour
50 g (2 oz) rolled oats
1 egg

For the topping
75 g (3 oz) plain or milk chocolate
25 g (1 oz) flaked almonds

1 Grease a shallow cake tin measuring about 18×28 cm (7×11 inches) and line the base with greaseproof paper. Cream together the butter, sugars, salt and vanilla essence until pale and fluffy. Sift in the flour, then add the oats and the egg. Beat everything together thoroughly.

2 Spread the mixture in the prepared tin and level the surface. Bake in the oven at 180°C (350°F) mark 4 for about 25 minutes or until well risen, lightly browned and shrinking away from the sides of the tin. Turn out and leave to cool on a wire rack.

3 Melt the chocolate (see page 12) and spread evenly on top of the biscuit. Sprinkle with the almonds and leave to set. Using a sharp knife, cut into about 16 bars.

DOUBLE CHOCOLATE CHUNK COOKIES

These are real American-style chocolate-packed cookies. Don't be surprised at the proportion of biscuit mixture to chocolate – it is correct!

MAKES ABOUT 14

50 g (2 oz) butter or margarine,
softened
50 g (2 oz) granulated sugar
40 g (1½ oz) light brown soft sugar
2.5 ml (½ tsp) vanilla essence
1 egg
125 g (4 oz) plain flour
1.25 ml (¼ level tsp) bicarbonate of
soda
1.25 ml (¼ level tsp) salt
175 g (6 oz) plain chocolate drops
175 g (6 oz) white chocolate,
chopped into large chunks
25 g (1 oz) pistachio nuts

1 Cream the butter until very soft. Add all the remaining ingredients, except the pistachios, and mix thoroughly.

2 Put about 14 large spoonfuls of the mixture, spaced well apart, on two large greased baking sheets. Press a few pistachio nuts into each spoonful. Bake in the oven at 180°C (350°F) mark 4 for 10–12 minutes or until the cookies are lightly tinged with brown. Do not overcook the biscuits; they should be soft in the centre. Leave on the baking sheets to cool for 10 minutes, then serve while warm or transfer to wire racks and leave to cool completely.

CHOCOLATE BISCUIT CAKE

A children's favourite!

SERVES 8

125 g (4 oz) plain or milk chocolate
15 ml (1 level tbsp) golden syrup
125 g (4 oz) butter or margarine
125 g (4 oz) digestive biscuits,
roughly broken up
25 g (1 oz) raisins or sultanas
25 g (1 oz) glacé cherries, halved
50 g (2 oz) flaked almonds, toasted

1 Butter a loose-bottomed 15–18 cm (6–7 inch) tin or ring.
2 Melt the chocolate (see page 12) with the syrup and butter.
3 When the chocolate and butter have melted, leave to cool slightly before stirring in the remaining ingredients.
4 Turn the mixture into the prepared tin, lightly level the top, then chill until set.

CHOCOLATE SHORTIES

Sprinkling the grated chocolate on to the biscuits as soon as they come out of the oven ensures that it sticks.

MAKES ABOUT 36

200 g (7 oz) self-raising flour
150 g (5 oz) caster sugar
1.25 ml (¼ level tsp) grated nutmeg
150 g (5 oz) butter or margarine
125 g (4 oz) ground almonds
50 g (2 oz) plain chocolate,
coarsely grated
1 egg, beaten

1 Grease three baking sheets. Sift the flour, sugar and nutmeg into a bowl, then rub in the butter until the mixture resembles fine breadcrumbs. Stir in the ground almonds and half the grated chocolate. Add the egg and mix together to form a dough.
2 Divide the mixture in half and roll each piece on a sheet of greaseproof paper or non-stick baking parchment into a 30.5 cm (12 inch) long, thin sausage shape.
3 Chill in the freezer or ice-making compartment of the refrigerator for about 30 minutes or until firm.
4 Cut each roll at an angle into about 18 slices and place well apart on the prepared baking sheets. Bake in the oven at 190°C (375°F) mark 5 for 15–20 minutes. Sprinkle with the remaining grated chocolate, then transfer to wire racks and leave to cool.

CHAPTER EIGHT

SAUCES, FROSTINGS AND ICINGS

BUTTER CREAM

Butter cream can be used as a filling or an icing.

MAKES 250 G (9 OZ)

75 g (3 oz) butter, softened
175 g (6 oz) icing sugar
a few drops of vanilla essence
15–30 ml (1–2 tbsp) milk or warm
water

1 Put the butter in a bowl and cream until very soft. Sift and gradually beat in the icing sugar, then add the vanilla essence and milk or water.
2 Spread the butter cream over the top of a cake only, or over the top and sides, using a palette knife or spatula. Decorate by making swirls in the butter cream or by marking with the prongs of a fork. Butter cream can also be piped.

Variations

Chocolate Dissolve 15 ml (1 level tbsp) cocoa powder in a little hot water and cool before adding to the mixture.

Mocha Dissolve 5 ml (1 level tsp) cocoa powder and 10 ml (2 level tsp) instant coffee granules in a little hot water taken from the measured amount. Cool before adding to the mixture.

Orange or Lemon Replace the vanilla essence with a little finely grated orange or lemon rind. Add a little juice from the fruit instead of the milk, beating well to avoid curdling the mixture.

Coffee Replace the vanilla essence with 10 ml (2 level tsp) instant coffee granules dissolved in some of the warm liquid; cool before adding to the mixture. Or replace 15 ml (1 tbsp) of the liquid with the same amount of coffee essence.

Almond Add 30 ml (2 level tbsp) finely chopped toasted almonds and mix thoroughly.

PERFECT CHOCOLATE GANACHE

This is the easiest and most foolproof method of making ganache, kindly taught to us by an experienced chocolatier. Use the very best chocolate for a really intense, bittersweet chocolate flavour.

Chocolate Ganache is wonderfully versatile. Use it warm as a sauce for ice cream or poached pears, and whenever a rich chocolate sauce is called for. If lightly chilled, chocolate ganache will thicken, then it may be used as a filling for meringues, gâteaux or choux buns.

SERVES ABOUT 8

400 g (14 oz) couverture chocolate
or 300 g (11 oz) plain chocolate
(see Note)
300 ml (½ pint) double cream

1 Using a large sharp knife, chop the chocolate into fairly small pieces and put it in a large heatproof bowl. Put the cream in a heavy-based saucepan and bring to the boil. Watch the cream carefully because it will rise up the pan and bubble over as it boils.
2 As soon as the cream boils, pour it over the chocolate. Leave, undisturbed, for 5 minutes.
3 Using a large balloon whisk, begin whisking the mixture gently, starting from the centre of the bowl and gradually incorporating all of the melted chocolate from the bottom. Serve while warm as a sauce, or leave to cool and thicken, and use as a filling.

Note

When using couverture chocolate it is possible to use a higher proportion of chocolate to cream because melted couverture is more viscous than 'ordinary' plain chocolate.

CHOCOLATE CUSTARD SAUCE

An everyday chocolate sauce to serve with steamed and baked puddings, pies and tarts.

MAKES 300 ML (½ PINT)

15 ml (1 level tbsp) cocoa powder
25 ml (1½ level tbsp) cornflour
about 25 ml (1½ level tbsp) caster
sugar, or to taste
300 ml (½ pint) milk

1 Blend the cocoa powder, cornflour and sugar to a smooth paste with a little of the milk.
2 In a heavy-based, preferably non-stick, saucepan, heat the remaining milk until almost boiling. Pour on to the cornflour mixture, stirring all the time. Return the mixture to the saucepan and bring to the boil, stirring continuously. Continue cooking for 2 minutes after the sauce has boiled. Add a little extra sugar to taste, if desired. Serve the sauce hot.

Variations

Chocolate Orange Custard Add the finely grated rind of 1 orange.
Coffee Custard Replace the cocoa powder with instant coffee granules.

CHOCOLATE FUDGE SAUCE

Serve this sticky fudge sauce with profiteroles, ice cream and bananas. In winter, add a tablespoonful of rum, brandy or liqueur to the finished sauce.

MAKES ABOUT 450 ML (¾ PINT)

75 ml (5 tbsp) single cream
25 g (1 oz) cocoa powder
125 g (4 oz) caster sugar
175 g (6 oz) golden syrup
25 g (1 oz) butter or margarine
a pinch of salt
2.5 ml (½ tsp) vanilla essence

1 Combine all the ingredients, except the vanilla essence, in a saucepan over low heat, and mix well. Slowly bring to the boil, stirring occasionally. Boil for 5 minutes, then add the vanilla essence.
2 Leave the hot fudge sauce to cool slightly before serving.

CHOCOLATE NUT BUTTER

Serve with hot pancakes and waffles or on toast.

SERVES 4

125 g (4 oz) butter, softened
10 ml (2 level tsp) caster sugar
30 ml (2 tbsp) grated chocolate
30 ml (2 tbsp) finely chopped
walnuts, hazelnuts or pecan nuts

Beat the butter until very light and fluffy, then beat in the remaining ingredients.

CRÈME ANGLAISE

Crème Anglaise is a lightly thickened 'real' custard, and makes a good accompaniment to some of our more special chocolate desserts. It's also the base for rich, creamy bavarois (set custard) and wonderful ice creams. It should be silky smooth with no sign of curdling, so it must never boil. It can be made in a double saucepan, but this is very slow. If you're careful using a saucepan, you'll have perfect custard every time.

SERVES 4

½ vanilla pod
300 ml (½ pint) milk
3 egg yolks
20 ml (4 level tsp) caster sugar

1 Split open the vanilla pod and scrape out the seeds into a medium, heavy-based saucepan. Add the pod and the milk. Bring slowly to the boil, take off the heat, cover and leave to infuse for 30 minutes. Remove the vanilla pod.

2 Place the egg yolks and sugar in a medium bowl. Using a balloon whisk, electric whisk or wooden spoon, beat the yolks and sugar until they lighten in colour and thicken slightly.

3 Pour the infused milk on to the mixture, whisking or stirring until evenly mixed. Rinse the saucepan, then return the mixture to the pan. Have ready a cold bowl with a sieve over the top.

4 Place the saucepan over a low to moderate heat and cook the custard for about 10 minutes, stirring all the time, until it thickens slightly and begins to coat the back of the spoon. Do not boil or the custard will curdle. (Watch the froth on the custard – when it begins to disappear, the custard is starting to thicken.)

5 Immediately strain the custard into the cold bowl to stop it cooking further. Whisk to reduce the temperature. To serve warm, pour into a jug. To serve cold, place damp greaseproof paper on the surface of the hot custard to prevent a skin forming, leave to cool, then chill.

Variations

Chocolate Omit the vanilla pod. Break up 50 g (2 oz) plain chocolate and bring it slowly to the boil with the milk, whisking until smooth. Complete as above, using 15 ml (1 level tbsp) sugar only.

Orange, Lemon or Mint Omit the vanilla pod. Add the pared rind of ½ a lemon or ½ an orange, or a handful of washed mint, to the milk and bring to the boil. Complete as above, straining the milk on to the egg yolks.

Nutmeg and Sherry Omit the vanilla pod. Prepare the custard as above, adding a dash of grated nutmeg and 15–30 ml (1–2 tbsp) sherry at the end.

Extra Creamy Replace half or all of the milk with single cream, or half single and half double cream.

Notes

It is important to rinse out the saucepan in step 3 before heating the mixture, to avoid the custard burning on to the base of the pan. If the custard begins to separate and look like runny scrambled eggs, it is curdling. To rescue it, strain it immediately into the cold bowl, add a few ice cubes and whisk vigorously to reduce the temperature – it should smooth out again quite quickly. If you are nervous of curdling the custard, beat 5 ml (1 level tsp) cornflour with the egg yolks in step 2. This helps thicken the custard, but taste it after cooking to ensure that all traces of cornflour have disappeared. If necessary, stir over a gentle heat for a little longer, but do not boil.

For convenience, a few drops of vanilla essence can replace the vanilla pod. Add to the milk at the beginning of step 3.

RASPBERRY COULIS

This fruity, vivid pink sauce is delicious with all manner of chocolate concoctions, and of course it's obligatory when serving a pudding 'nouvelle' style. We particularly liked it with Chocolate Roulade (see page 86), Chocolate Heaven (see page 106), or White Chocolate and Sherry Mousse (see page 97) and almost any frozen chocolate pudding. Don't be tempted to add too much sugar; remember that the chocolate mixture is likely to be quite sweet.

SERVES 4

225 g (8 oz) fresh raspberries
icing sugar, to taste
a splash of your favourite liqueur
(optional)

1 Purée the raspberries in a blender or food processor, then push through a nylon sieve to remove the seeds. If the raspberries are very ripe, it may be possible simply to push them through a sieve to purée them.
2 Add icing sugar to taste, then stir in a little liqueur, if using. Serve cold.

FRESH ORANGE SAUCE

Serve with Double Chocolate Ice Cream (see page 113). Blood oranges give the best colour.

SERVES 4

6 oranges, preferably blood oranges
10 ml (2 level tsp) cornflour
25 g (1 oz) caster sugar

1 With a swivel potato peeler, thinly pare the rind from one orange and set aside. Squeeze the juice from all the oranges into a measuring jug and make up to 300 ml (½ pint) with water if necessary. Strain into a small saucepan. Blend the cornflour to a smooth paste with 30 ml (2 tbsp) water and stir into the orange juice with the sugar.
2 Bring the sauce slowly to the boil, stirring continuously. Simmer until slightly thickened and clear, then pour into a bowl, cover loosely and set aside to cool.
3 Cut the reserved orange rind into needle-thin shreds. Drop into a saucepan of boiling water, then simmer for 3–4 minutes or until tender. Drain and cool under cold water, then add to the sauce. Serve cold.

CRÈME AU BEURRE

Use this rich butter cream to fill chocolate sponges, Swiss rolls and gâteaux.

MAKES ABOUT 275 G (10 OZ)

75 g (3 oz) caster sugar
2 egg yolks, beaten
175 g (6 oz) butter, softened

1 Place the sugar in a heavy-based sauce-pan, add 60 ml (4 tbsp) water and heat very gently to dissolve the sugar, without boiling.
2 When the sugar is completely dissolved, bring to the boil and boil steadily for 2–3 minutes, to reach a temperature of 107°C (225°F). (Check the temperature on a sugar thermometer.)
3 Pour the syrup in a thin stream on to the egg yolks in a deep bowl, whisking all the time. Continue to whisk until the mixture is thick and cold.
4 In another bowl, cream the butter until very soft and gradually beat in the egg yolk mixture.

Variations

Chocolate Melt 50 g (2 oz) plain chocolate with 15 ml (1 tbsp) water (see page 14). Cool slightly and beat into the Crème au Beurre mixture.
Fruit Crush 225 g (8 oz) fresh strawberries, raspberries, etc., or thaw, drain and crush frozen fruit. Beat into the Crème au Beurre mixture.
Orange or Lemon Add freshly grated rind and juice to taste to the Crème au Beurre mixture.
Coffee Beat 15–30 ml (1–2 tbsp) coffee essence into the Crème au Beurre mixture.

CHOCOLATE FUDGE FROSTING

MAKES ENOUGH TO FILL AND COVER THE TOP OF A 20.5 CM (8 INCH) CAKE

50 g (2 oz) butter
125 g (4 oz) soft brown sugar
75 g (3 oz) plain chocolate, broken into pieces
30 ml (2 tbsp) single cream
200 g (7 oz) icing sugar, sifted

1 Put the butter, sugar, chocolate and cream in a saucepan.
2 Heat gently until the sugar has dissolved, then bring to the boil and boil briskly for 3 minutes.
3 Remove from the heat and gradually stir in the icing sugar. Beat until smooth, using a wooden spoon, and continue to beat for about 2 minutes or until the icing is thick enough to spread. Use immediately, spreading with a wet palette knife.

SEVEN-MINUTE FROSTING

MAKES ABOUT 175 G (6 OZ)

1 egg white
175 g (6 oz) caster sugar
a pinch of salt
a pinch of cream of tartar

1 Put the ingredients in a heatproof bowl with 30 ml (2 tbsp) water. Whisk lightly.
2 Place the bowl over a pan of hot water and heat, whisking continuously, until the mixture thickens sufficiently to stand in peaks. This will take about 7 minutes.
3 Pour the frosting over the top of the cake and spread with a palette knife.

SUPPLIERS

Harrods
Huge comprehensive chocolate department. Delivery and mail order services.

87 Brompton Road
Knightsbridge
London SW1X 7XL
Tel: 071-730 1234

Squires Kitchen
Marvellous range of specialist sweet- and cake-making ingredients and equipment: chocolate moulds, gold leaf, gold flake, sweet papers, couverture chocolate, cake tins. Catalogue available. Mail order service.

3 Waverley Lane
Farnham
Surrey GU9 8BB
Tel: 0252-711749

B.R. Mathews and Sons
Fantastic range of cake tins and boards, cake decorations, icing and decorating equipment, chocolate moulds, bakers' chocolate, couverture chocolate, chocolate drops, Easter egg moulds and boxes, petit four cases. Catalogue available. Mail order service.

12 Gypsy Hill
Upper Norwood
London SE10 1NN
Tel: 081-670 0788

Woodnutts
Specialist bakeware, icing equipment, couverture chocolate, turntables. Catalogue available. Mail order service.

97 Church Road
Hove
East Sussex BN3 2BA
Tel: 0273-205353

Le Croque Monsieur
Couverture chocolate.

251 Otley Road
West Park
Leeds LS16 5LQ
Tel: 0532-787353

David Mellor
Comprehensive range of cook's equipment including cake tins, biscuit cutters, icing equipment, chocolate moulds, Easter egg moulds, dipping forks. Catalogue available. Mail order service.

4 Sloane Square
London SW1W 8EE
Tel: 071-730 4259

22 Shad Thames
Butlers Wharf
London SE1 2YU
Tel: 071-407 7593

66 King Street
Manchester M2 4NP
Tel: 061-834 7023

Divertimenti
Comprehensive range of baking ware and moulds, chocolate pots, icing and cake-decorating equipment, chocolate moulds. Catalogue available. For mail order service contact Wigmore Street branch.

45–47 Wigmore Street
London W1H 9LE
Tel: 071-935 0689

139–141 Fulham Road
South Kensington
London SW1 6SD
Tel: 071-581 8065

Corteil and Barratt
Cake boards, cake-decorating equipment, plain, milk and white couverture chocolate, sweet boxes, dipping forks, chocolate moulds, foil sweet papers, fondant fillings.

40 High Street
Ewell Village
Surrey
Tel: 081-393 0032

Sugarworks
Couverture chocolate, chocolate moulds, sweet boxes.

161 Lower High Street
Stourbridge
West Midlands
Tel: 0384-442075

Lakeland Plastics
Gold paper sweet cases. Catalogue available. Mail order service.

Alexandra Building
Windermere
Cumbria LA23 15Q
Tel: 05394 88100

The Souvenir & Decorations Co.
Bags, ribbons and sweet boxes. Catalogue available. Mail order service.

Soudeco House
1a Aldenham Road
Watford
Herts WD1 4AD
Tel: 0923 817227

ACKNOWLEDGEMENTS

We would like to thank the following: Carrie Groom of the Porter Chocolate Company for her help and words of wisdom; the entire staff of *Good Housekeeping* magazine (especially Emma Wiggin and the subs and art departments) for their unfailing eagerness to consume our chocolate creations; Moyra Fraser, Caroline Walker, Fiona Hunter, Riley Stemp, Sarah Edmunds, Kate Fryer, Carla Newman and Camilla Stevens – the entire *Good Housekeeping* Cookery Department – for forgetting their diets for the duration of the recipe testing; Helen Casey for being a great help and Sylvia Stephenson for her help scraping set chocolate off the GHI kitchen work surfaces!
We would also like to thank James Murphy, Roísín Nield, Tom and Nat for the yummy photographs, and Sander Architectural Mirrors, Sander House, Elmore Street, London N1.
Finally, special thanks to Julia Thorpe.

INDEX